Sumaa Tekur is a writer and editor with stints in publications like *The Times of India*, *Deccan Herald*, *Femina*, and *DNA*. She has also contributed to various British dailies and holds a Masters in International Journalism from City University, London. Her spiritual journey started early in life and this quest gained momentum with solo travelling, which gave her many opportunities for rich learning, reflection, and time to construct her own unique framework of spirituality. She offers this unique perspective in her spiritual consultancy, Golden Swan Healing (www.goldenswanhealing.com), through which she supports many a new and seasoned seeker.

Sumaa lives in Bengaluru with her books, paints and canvases, lamps, and drums. Her solitude is shared only with the mango tree next to her window, her stable, all-weather companion.

THE INNER LIGHT

A Beginner's Guide to Spirituality & Finding Peace

SUMAA TEKUR

HAY HOUSE

Hay House Publishers India

Australia • India

United Kingdom • United States

Hay House Publishers (India) Pvt. Ltd.
Muskaan Complex, Plot No.3, B-2 Vasant Kunj, New Delhi-110 070, India
Hay House Inc., PO Box 5100, Carlsbad, CA 92018-5100, USA
Hay House UK, Ltd., The Sixth Floor, Watson House, 54 Baker Street, W1U 7BU, UK
Hay House Australia Pty Ltd., 18/36 Ralph St., Alexandria NSW 2015, Australia
Email: contact@hayhouse.co.in
www.hayhouse.co.in

ISBN 978-93-91067-54-0
ISBN 978-93-91067-77-9 (e-book)

Printed at Repro India Limited

To
Chikkappa (Dr Shirdi Prasad Tekur),
Empath and healing ninja. Your inner light glowed
with the secret of life.

To
Ma and Pa, for putting up with me.
I am because you are.

Contents

Introduction 9

1. Finding Your Personal Brand of Spirituality 13
2. Spirituality—Types and its True Meaning 27
3. Exploring Spirituality 43
4. How to Start Meditating 61
5. The Guru and the Cult 79
6. Navigating the Vast Spirituality Seas 101
7. The Material and the Spiritual 117
8. Creativity—Where the Material and the Spiritual Meet 133
9. Exploring Spirituality through Sexuality 149
10. Religion and Spirituality 159
11. The Role of Rituals in Spirituality 175
12. The Pilgrimage 189
13. The Social Spirituals 197
14. Spiritual Values and Activism 213
15. The Isolation Myth 229

Conclusion 245

Author's Thanks 249

Without going out of my door
I can know all things on Earth
Without looking out of my window
I could know the ways of Heaven
The farther one travels
The less one knows
The less one really knows

Without going out of your door
You can know all things on Earth
Without looking out of your window
You could know the ways of Heaven
The farther one travels
The less one knows
The less one really knows

Arrive without travelling
See all without looking
Do all without doing

—The Inner Light, The Beatles

Introduction

Two people walked into the London Heathrow airport lounge and occupied individual sofa-seaters near where I sat reading a book. The first was a 60-plus woman who was visibly harassed by the cancellation of her connecting flight. She would now have to not only wait longer but also take a circuitous route with another connection at New York to reach her destination.

The second person, a gentleman in his late thirties, was dressed sharply in a black suit and had a soft smile as he casually looked around. When our eyes met, we realised that we had both been people-watching. We struck up a conversation and found out that we were on the same flight that was cancelled and were waiting to be listed on another flight.

As we spoke, I was pleasantly surprised to learn that he held a senior position in a prime global company. It intrigued me that he didn't carry the aura of stress and the burden of decision-making that most people in his position generally wore. He travelled business class but liked to mingle in crowded airport lounges as it helped him to stay connected to the people, he told me. He clearly wasn't perturbed by the delay in his arrival in the United States although it would upset his meeting plans. He shrugged and said: 'There's more to life than meetings and there's definitely more to life than the corner office.' His eyes twinkled as he said those words. In that moment, I felt a surge of respect for this man that I barely knew. Only a deep-rooted hold on one's personal values can keep a man from succumbing to temptations of power and the heady rush of success in an artificially erected social structure built on bricks of gold.

When I finally boarded my connecting flight to New York, the harassed 60-year-old lady sat a row behind me. She continued her conversations on the phone. I eavesdropped and learned that she was going to Chicago to teach a module on mindfulness and meditation at a conference. And she was upset that she, now, didn't have an evening to sleep off the jet lag. The missed flight had frazzled her nerves more than she could handle.

I found myself smiling at the synchronicity that brought these two people near me in the airport lounge. In those few hours, I had learned that spirituality is hardly about visible symbols—burning incense, saintly robes, folded hands, and closed eyes. It is so much about what we cannot see—calm in chaos, choosing peace over conflict, practising compassion, kindness in everyday interactions, inner balance, and widening life perspective.

Spirituality is all this and so much more. It is simple, and yet seems so complex. It is, perhaps, this paradoxical nature of spirituality that intimidates some of us who would love to integrate it into daily life but don't know how to engage with it.

The psychology of branding has entered the world of spirituality, too, taking it further away from its essence. If you could imagine the entire spiritual market displayed on a single supermarket aisle, it would be an unending line of branded products from gurus of various schools and provenance. These branded products would teach how to attain salvation, how to meditate, and how to master the mind. The gurus would also include, in their schools, everyday consumer products like groceries, toiletries, stationery, and even home décor stamped with a spiritual organisation's branding. Marketing brains join hands with spiritual teachers to express the seeker's loyalty for a guru in everyday shopping choices.

This book is for beginners looking to dip their toes, and then some, into the waters of spirituality without getting caught in the whirlpool of spiritual consumerism. The book answers the question: How can I walk this path with awareness to improve my understanding of life?

It's for those of us who ask: Where do I even start? What is spirituality? Why does it feel like to be spiritual is akin to climbing a steep mountain? This book tells you why it isn't like climbing a steep mountain and why you are, probably, climbing up the wrong mountain if you feel that way in your practice. And even though the mountain may not be steep, you will still likely meet your Shadow—the challenges that you need to overcome—along the climb. This Shadow, which can appear in the form of doubt, fear, control, illusion, delusion, and more, is not to be feared. It is, after all, a part of you. We can only grow if we become more aware of our Shadow and how it makes us behave. Walking the spiritual path is also about this learning and improved awareness.

I am not affiliated to any spiritual group, organisation, or guru. And this, I believe, puts me in a unique position to share examples and perspectives about leading a spiritual life, drawn from personal encounters, and from the experiences shared by fellow seekers.

The book tackles questions about spirituality and religion, material life, family dharma, the importance of a guru, cult, activism, and so much more. While it is designed for beginners on this path by offering doses of confidence through shared stories and insights from seekers, even those who have been on the path for a few years might find these insights equally useful. After all, one often needs to return to the basics to ensure that the foundation is a perfectly paved runway for take-off.

This is not a book that recommends spiritual paths or reviews organisations and gurus. But it does tell readers what to expect while wading through the many possibilities and spiritual crossroads. In that, it is a friend and fellow seeker that you should take along with you on this exhilarating ride.

Here's wishing you a happy and fruitful spiritual journey.

1

Finding Your Personal Brand of Spirituality

'If light is in your heart, you will find your way home.'

—Rumi

SPIRITUALITY IS THE PROCESS OF SWITCHING ON YOUR inner light . . . and leaving it on.

Kartik listened to the views of his topmost trusted advisors as they sat in the online meeting brainstorming ways to navigate the looming recession with minimum loss to the company. Kartik, the founder and chief decision-maker at this medium-sized enterprise, his labour of love, took notes as he listened intently.

When the meeting concluded, Kartik reviewed the notes he had typed on the computer once again. In it, he had created a table with these headers:

1. What is in my control?
2. What isn't in my control?
3. What must I be prepared to let go?
4. What are my top 3 focus areas in the recovery period?
5. Reminders

Under the first three headers, Kartik listed the business outcomes and the company's best possible responses while bearing in mind both profit and human emotions. The last two headers were reiterating Kartik's daily actions to keep his own mental strength fit and fighting. His reminders included meditation, time with family, and time for hobbies and reading. These were built into his daily routine, and if these were normal circumstances, Kartik didn't need reminders. But these were extraordinary circumstances. In the rush to save his business, Kartik didn't want to let go of the most important behaviours that kept him strong at this time of crisis.

With hundreds of employees and their families dependent on his leadership, Kartik knew all too well the burden of responsibility. He could shoulder the blame and absorb the failure of not being able to keep up the promise that every leader makes while starting a company with stars in his eyes. Or he could do his best to be a fair and just leader while surrendering all which is not in his control.

Kartik chose the latter. And this choice wasn't an overnight response to his circumstances. He had been practising the art of letting go every day over years of meditation and through years of journaling his thoughts to separate the wheat from the chaff.

He would wake up at 5:00 a.m., no matter where in the world he was, to get 30 minutes of quiet time for himself before the day started. In this time, he meditated, thought only about his mental well-being, and journaled his thoughts to heighten awareness of his emotions, relationships, and situations.

This persistent daily activity may have seemed too repetitive and of not much use at the time but, today, Kartik was able to cash in on this behaviour to tide over a crisis. The daily meaningful reflections now enabled him to rely on his emotional and mental strength and on his intuition to make bold choices about the future of his company as well. His intention was clear—to take along as many people forward with him as he could. He stepped forward with this intention and the path appeared.

Kartik had to choose one out of many available choices. He had to deal with uncertainty and anxiety, his own and also that of his employees. When his external circumstances demanded so much of him, Kartik had the strength to focus on his internal world to draw energy from it and make decisions in the external world.

In fine, in his most trying of times, Kartik was relying on his inner light to lead him.

The stillness and calm that he had practised all these years came in handy when Kartik was able to respond to the crisis rather than simply react to it. He didn't lose his temper during the difficult weeks. Nobody else in his team or at home had to bear the brunt of his emotional distress. (Yes, he did feel the distress but was able to manage it. When it got difficult, he reached out for professional help.) Kartik was able to set clear intentions for the immediate future and weather the storm because his raincoat, the trusted intuition, would protect him.

This knowing, which came from his inner light, enabled him to read his current situation—not the future—clearly. Kartik had practised the art of managing daily stress by infusing his spirit with the arts. A music aficionado, he made time for activities beyond work even in the most time-stressed situations. He had learned how to take the pressure off work by indulging his love for music. Kartik knew that if he spent even a little time practising music, getting lost in the world of *ragas* (moods in music), he would always return to his work refreshed, ready to solve the problems with a fresh perspective.

This balanced lifestyle empowered Kartik with the necessary skills to trust that this is not the end of the world. And even if it were, it would be quite all right.

It wasn't an easy ride till here though. In his young

entrepreneurship days, Kartik struggled to keep up with this balance. But he persisted without giving up. Giving up would have been easy to do when the pressure of deadlines and targets pushed him to tackle the urgent while postponing the important. The truth is that there will always be something more urgent in the world of business that is waiting to wrestle your time away from a leisure pursuit. Kartik gave music a place of pride in his life, and it paid him back in many ways that cannot be quantified.

Kartik practised the art of balance, always staying at the centre of his life and, like a squirrel, hiding away seeds in different parts of his life—be it spirituality, business, the arts, or human relationships. He watered them every day, too. He didn't have great ambitions for how these seeds would grow, but this was the only way he knew to lead a full life.

And now, in his fifties, he was balancing life with finesse and knew that everything was equally important. At the same time, life cannot be only about one of these aspects. It is not only about business. It is not only about marriage. It is not only about music. Life is everything *together*, all at once. Kartik had cracked this paradox of life—working with dispassion and moderation in everything to taste joy and excellence.

Kartik's inner light was aglow through consistent practice of meditation and awareness of spirituality. And this light led him down a fulfilling life path of rich experiences. The highs and lows of material life, or spiritual life for that matter, couldn't shake his enthusiasm to take the next step forward . . . to continue welcoming each day with the curiosity to know what lies at the other end. His inner light shined the spotlight on the way forward.

Spirituality, Defined

Spirituality is the process of switching on your inner light.

It's only when the light is on that you can see clearly, both within and outside. And when you can see clearly, you can make changes for the better to lead a life that is in harmony and in alignment with your purpose.

By engaging with spirituality, you are learning how to access your inner light, turn on the switch, and let the glow of the light fill you up and spill to the world outside.

Here's the thing about spiritual work: It is a deeply personal and individual process. No one can tell you where the switch is hidden to turn on your inner light; you must look for it yourself. Nor can anyone tell you how to turn on the switch; you must discover for yourself how to operate it. Lastly, no one can tell you how to ensure that the light stays on; you must figure that out yourself, too.

In this process of finding your light, you can discover that there are things blocking your inner light from burning at its brightest. Spirituality teaches the process of parting the blinds and uncovering the blocks preventing your inner light from shining forth. You also learn to work with the shadows that this light leaves. Shadows are those parts of our inner selves that appear in the form of, for instance, low self-esteem, ego, envy, greed, anger, and other deleterious qualities, while the light manifests in the form of pure love, compassion, and kindness.

Spirituality, although a deeply personal process, also changes the way you interact with the world. Your inner light can begin to recognise the inner light in others. When in harmony, you are able to have healthy relationships with such people whose inner light glows in kindred luminosity with your own. Any exchange with people and your outer world then becomes a reflection of how your own inner light radiates.

When the inner light shines bright, not only do your eyes glow from its reflection, the light radiates to your outer world in a way that it reaches every person that you cross paths with. When you interact with another person whose inner light is also aglow, the exchange becomes fruitful, and both parties come away feeling blissful and elated. When the inner light is on, your exchanges with people always come from a place of calm knowing.

What's important to know is that you, like everyone else, have an inherent light that already exists. Spirituality is all about your engagement with your own light. It is the process of groping in the dark to find the light switch, learning how to operate the switch, dealing with the flood of light and the new awareness it creates once it is on, discovering a transformed existence—thanks to a clear vision from the light—and also working on forming a long-term relationship with your light.

The process of spirituality is really about 'finding your light' and making it shine.

Spirituality at the Sports Bar

On a solo weekend trip from London, I was seated at a bar in Geneva's historic Old Town, casually people-watching and enjoying a well-deserved pint after a long trek in the Swiss countryside. The bartender, Sergei, struck up a conversation and shared his story of travelling through Europe. He was from Eastern Europe and wanted to see the world when he was young and able. So, he backpacked through the continent and, to fund his travel, he took up odd jobs wherever he went.

Sergei had a ready smile that was not a fake service smile. He also had a witty comeback in casual conversations with most of the guests at the bar. Curious about his life, I asked him several questions about his ambitions, purpose, and aspirations. He initially joked about wanting to build a castle made of gold and marry the richest woman on earth. But as the evening stretched, between serving drinks to patrons, he opened up about his life.

Sergei said that he had no lofty ambitions or goals. All he wanted was to live just for today. He took one day at a time, not even planning too far ahead. He was going to be in Geneva for a couple of months and then he wasn't sure about his next destination. Although Sergei had wanderer's feet, at heart, he was always at home. He wasn't moving in search of anything specific. He was simply being present to a wide range of experiences that this big, exciting world had to offer.

He was focused on becoming a better person. His meditation was to travel the world and find the calmest places where he could hear nothing but the sounds of nature. He would go in search of waterfalls, forests, mountaintops, and rivers to simply sit in companionable silence with nature. This was his idea of meditation. . . of investing in the Self. It was his therapy, devised by his own style.

His worldview was unlike anything I had heard of or experienced till then. What he said next truly opened my mind to the idea of spirituality. 'I want to leave everyone who crosses my path better off than before. You never know what someone is going through. Just be nice to people. And it will go around the world like a big bear hug,' he said, or something to that effect.

The first thought that came to my mind when I heard Sergei say these words was that he was truly spiritual. In those few hours at the bar, I had seen how Sergei had made every person who came to the bar smile. And just like that, he was making the world a kinder place. Kindness was his personal brand of spirituality.

Spirituality, Redefined

In my earliest interactions with people who were generally known to be spiritual, I couldn't visibly spot their spiritual inclination. Sure, they seemed to smile a lot and sit quietly doing nothing, watching people, and being nonintrusive. But their spirituality was not a physical armour that they wore proudly on the sleeve.

Moreover, I never thought of the distinction between being spiritual or religious. It is only now, decades later, after gaining some basic understanding of the subject do I recognise those who carry the torch of spirituality all the time. Such people stand out from the crowd. Their eyes shine with a beautiful knowing.

When I was growing up, I understood religion and spirituality synonymously, as do most people. If a person wasn't perceptibly religious, I believed that she wasn't spiritual. My understanding of it all changed at that bar in Geneva, which tested everything that I thought I knew about spirituality.

I had to redefine it to better understand its many nuances. Here is a list of those beliefs. They are, by no measure, exhaustive but are a good start to step inside the door and break the mystic aura that the word spirituality carries:

1. **I always believed that spirituality was linked to religion.** Sergei was an agnostic and believed that religion wasn't going to be his path. Sure, he spent

time at monasteries if the environment there felt welcoming and if he was instinctively drawn to it. But a religion-led life wasn't his calling, and he had realised this very early in life. His lack of interest in religion did not interfere in his spiritual aspirations.

2. **I believed that spiritual people were older and had a wise aura about them.** To this, I can only laugh today at my naivety. Spirituality has nothing to do with age. The years may add some patience and wisdom to our actions and relationships but this, alone, doesn't make us spiritual.
3. **I believed that spiritual people dressed a certain way**, wearing long, flowing robes or carrying prayer beads or speaking in soft tones, using arcane words. For a very long time, I associated spirituality with two extremes—the traditional religious priests and the hippies. Not necessarily, I learned. Only after meeting Sergei did I realise that spirituality had nothing to do with clothes and appearance. Sergei was your average Joe who broke the mould of appearance, having nothing to do with who you are as a person. This was one of my bigger beliefs that were challenged.
4. **I believed that spirituality was to be found in certain physical places like in front of the altar, at a temple or church, or in an ashram.** Sergei was being spiritual anywhere and everywhere, and that day, at a sports bar. He went out into nature and found his spirituality there. He found spirituality in the train, in the ice-cream store, at the beer bar, and while walking in a museum. He defined spirituality for himself and lived it location-agnostic, as a chosen lifestyle.

5. **I believed that spirituality was an organised, linear set of rules with meditation at its heart.** Sergei had figured out his own personal spirituality. His meditation was along with nature and had little to do with posture, place, time, or breath. He was tuning in to his immediate environment in meditation. His inner light was aglow to this awareness.
6. **I believed that spirituality was a serious pursuit that involved long hours of deep meditation, silence and struggle, even renunciation.** In Sergei's case, humour motivated his spirituality. He wanted to laugh and make the world laugh. His spirituality certainly started there, at a point that was accessible and manageable to him on an everyday level.
7. **I believed that spirituality was all about inaction.** I believed that it was about sitting still, going inward, and reflecting. But that was only one aspect of spirituality, which was switching on the inner light. That light then spilled outside. Sergei was managing the reflection of his inner light by travelling, constantly moving, and immersing in qualitative, sensual life experiences that demanded complete surrender.
8. **I believed that spirituality was impractical in a practical world.** My idea of spirituality was that one had to be philosophical and give everything deep thought. I also thought that one had to renounce the material world, become a monk, and sit in introspection and meditation for life. When I saw how Sergei lived it up, I understood that spirituality could only be useful if it is practical. Spirituality is not an either/or with life. Spirituality pervades all

of life itself. And it is up to each of us to choose the brand of spirituality that we subscribe to—kindness, compassion, service, love, and humour besides so many more values.

9. **I believed that spirituality was inward-looking, mainly by working on one's inner self.** But I saw Sergei's commitment to making the world a better place in whatever way he could. He believed in spreading joy with smiles and humour. He volunteered for the environment wherever he travelled. He wasn't passive but an active spiritualist.
10. **I believed that spirituality was not for everyone; it was only for the 'spiritual types'.** I defined 'spiritual types' as the ones who had undergone serious trauma and needed deep healing. Sergei didn't fit into the stereotype that I had held in my mind of who needed spiritual guidance. I understood that spirituality was for everyone. Each of us has our own way of switching on our inner light, whatever that takes. But it is for *everyone.*
11. **I believed that spirituality was about escaping the world briefly; that's why the spiritually inclined meditated.** Sergei taught me that spiritual people engaged with the world around them. They were ever conscious, aware, and ready to respond to situations as needed. They were not people who sat in a bubble and meditated to levitate from the world and its problems.
12. **I believed that spiritual people were lonely and are used to being alone.** I believed that spiritual practice took social connections away from your life and

> isolated you so that you could focus on it solely. This could not be farthest from the truth. Sergei had friends everywhere he travelled. He relied on contacts to decide where to travel next, which freelance gig to find, and where to shack up for a few months. All this didn't take anything away from his personal spirituality. If anything, his fellowship grew with his cheer and positivity.

In just that one evening, with that one chance meeting, my understanding of spirituality began to look very different. Suddenly, spirituality was fun. It was accessible; it was friendly and, what's more, I understood that I could make it whatever I wanted it to be for me. I was excited to find out what my spirituality would look like.

I am sure that there are millions out there who follow their own brand of spirituality that has no title or structure. One such story that challenged my previously held idea of spirituality is from the popular book *Shantaram* by Gregory David Roberts whose visit to India and its slums transformed his world view. While Sergei was pursuing his spirituality in the open amidst the woods, bird calls, and whistling winds, Gregory's experiences in India helped him connect the spiritual links while he was in a prison cell, writing draft after draft of his mega masterpiece, *Shantaram*.

And there you have it. Spirituality can be triggered at any place, it can be nurtured under any circumstances, and it can make a world of difference simply because you make your own rules. It is deeply personal. Someone else can only share their experience. But you have to walk your own road and find your personal brand of spirituality.

2

Spirituality—
Types and its True Meaning

'We carry inside us the wonders we seek outside us.'

—Rumi

WAIT, THERE ARE TYPES?

No. Not really. Based loosely on the entry point, spirituality is often understood through the lens of religion, human values, philosophy, or a core belief. There is Hinduism-, Buddhism-, and Judaism-based spirituality. There is service-led spirituality, which preaches the idea of expressing love for humanity through giving. There is also mindfulness-based spirituality, which is all about the philosophy of bringing about greater mindfulness into everything that we do, whether it is eating, reading, writing, sitting, or singing. These are all, of course, loose terms and definitions.

These types also overlap. For example, although religion-based spirituality is cloaked in rituals, and structure is of paramount importance, it can be an effective way to also follow mindfulness. This is done by encouraging seekers to improve their discipline of the mind and body with the goal of leading a healthier way of life. The role of religion in using multiple ways to encourage seekers to turn on their inner light is significant.

There are other ways of understanding spirituality, too. One way is to be led by the value of universal oneness, in which the practice is centred on the idea that we are all the same. And from this core philosophy, an entire lifestyle and thought- and behaviour-pattern emerges. This, too, can bring about huge change in the way we think and act, most predominantly, by reiterating that we are all one.

To further categorise the practices, any brand of spirituality could be said to follow the three clusters mentioned below.

Somatic Spirituality

Simply put, this type of spiritual work is all about the body. The body is the house, vehicle, and seat of our lives. It is the carrier of our experiences and emotions. Bringing greater awareness to the body and working with it can, in itself, be a spiritual process.

There are several ways of doing this bodywork, as it is termed in modern parlance. The first and most obvious method is to focus on the breath and feel the pulse—that most tangible symbol of life. In yogic practice, this is called Pranayama. In more modern spiritual and healing terminology, it is called breathwork, referring to a range of ways in which we can consciously control the breath with the aim of promoting better mental and emotional health.

The physical body is a storehouse of wisdom. Often, when pushed through stressful situations, the anxiety has a way of bypassing the logical mind and taking a seat in different parts of the body. The heart, for example, could store grief. The liver could be a seat of anger, and the kidney could be a home for unexpressed desires, all sparing the conscious mind from processing this trauma.

Physical illnesses are the body's way of screaming for attention. Listening to the body and making a habit of tending to its needs is a form of self-care. Caring for the body creates awareness and mindfulness, which can be achieved by awakening the body. This can be done in many ways.

One of the most ancient and widely accepted somatic spiritual practices is yoga. I like to describe yoga as a conversation with the body, in which the mind does more of the listening and the body does more of the talking. When we stretch, squeeze, bend, and fold our bodies, we test its limits and understand how it feels. When we open the chest outward, we know how comfortable we are with sharing our deepest fears and desires. When we fold the chest and bend inward, we realise how much we truly are in touch with our inner selves.

Some schools of thought believe that talking to the body directly, whether it is to a sprained ankle, a hurt elbow, or even a heart that has undergone bypass surgery, can be greatly effective in healing. It's not complicated, really. It is simply about talking to the body part that is carrying the pain. This practice brings awareness to how we treat and respect our bodies. One self-care routine that is known to also improve self-esteem is to look in the mirror and tell ourselves that we are beautiful. Say it enough times and you begin to believe it, if you don't already.

Many classical dances are a creative form of spiritual self-expression that use body movements for a holistic body, mind, and spiritual connection. *Mudras* (hand gestures) are a type of bodywork to orchestrate the energy flow. The whirling dervishes in Sufism are a strongly spiritual somatic experience in which the entire physical act of trance-like whirling is a meditation in dance. The dancers wear white robes to represent the shroud of ego and chant while twirling with arms open to embrace all of humanity and God's love.

One of the urban physical fitness trends that has held steady globally over the decades has to be marathon running. The body tests the brutal limits of its physical stamina while the mind knocks on the doors of willpower. The body and mind have to work in tandem for a runner to complete a marathon. When one feels weak, the other has to step up. Japanese writer Haruki Murakami has described this mind-body collaboration in his inimitably brilliant style in the book *What I Talk About When I Talk About Running*. This autobiographical account of Murakami's marathon experiences reveals the spirituality of donning running shoes and hitting the streets for hours of running with nothing but your thoughts to keep you company. It is meditation in motion.

Another form of somatic spiritual experience is purification of the body through fasting and sense withdrawal. Every major religion of the world has some form of fasting and withdrawal built into its philosophy. It is believed that any disciplining of the body is great preparation for mind control. Physical exercise has uses beyond fitness and body management. It is a preparation for us to be able to sit in meditation for at least 30 minutes. Every day is a practice to prepare the body for greater mind control and concentration.

Fasting and deprivation is a way to grow willpower and give the mind a stronger grip on thoughts and actions. The fasting can be of anything that we consume. Today, intermittent fasting is a raging global trend but ancient traditions already had this format of eating built into the idea of a healthy lifestyle. Similarly, abstinence from sex and alcohol are considered to be preparation for mind control while moving towards a simpler consumption format—the idea being that the less we put into our body, the lighter it becomes.

The body is a road map to our emotions, intuitions, desires, and memories. If we learn how to read this map, it leads to greater self-awareness and, ultimately, healing.

Psychological Practices

While somatic experiences bring more attention and awareness to the body, psychological practices, as the name suggests, are all about the mind. This type of spirituality is all about disciplining and controlling the mind.

Working with the mind starts with learning how to concentrate. The basic problem with this is that we're not taught how to concentrate. We're told to concentrate but not taught the steps that truly go into reining in the mind and making it focus on a point or object without distraction. A wide range of psychological practices revolving around meditation attempt to teach us how to do this.

At the very root, psychological practices bring our awareness to what we think about, how we think, where the mind travels, and how to bring the mind to think about, or not to think about, something.

Meditation is often given as a blanket solution to all and any of life's problems. But it is not easy to learn how to meditate. The monkey mind flits from one thought to the next to the next, making it difficult to spend even ten minutes in meditation. But intent and practise go a long way to work with the mind.

Under psychological practices are also the acts of chanting and *japa* (repetitive mantra recitation), which is, again, designed to focus the mind on the chants. Mantra japa is a balm to an overactive mind. Conscious and mindful chanting reduces overthinking and the stresses caused by mental anxieties and worries. In some schools of thought, mantra japa is also said to reduce the karmic intensity accumulated over lifetimes. Sitting in recitation is said to erase, at least, some karmic baggage, in that you are not accumulating more karma while sitting in chanting sessions.

Within the four folds of the yogic practice, raja yoga is the study of the human mind. The mind observes itself—where it travels, how it triggers memories, what it thinks of someone or something, etc. This observation and study of the mind makes us increasingly aware of its tendencies. Is the mind moving towards jealousy? Is it promoting hatred? Is it falling in love? Is it slipping down a negative spiral?

Reflection, contemplation, and introspective thinking are ways to achieve any mind-understanding goals. Journal writing is a proven, deep-thinking process that slows down the brain to analyse a situation, our response, and how we think. It takes practice and intent, of course, to be completely honest with ourselves about what we really think of something or someone. But this is also part of the mind's journey and a deeply spiritual exercise.

Social Spirituality

The first two types described above work with the body and mind to create a holistic internal spiritual experience. The third type looks outward wherein the seeker works with her environment as a way of increasing awareness about the outer world and allowing that awareness to translate inward, too.

Service is central to this school of thought. Through social service, the seeker becomes more aware of the world around her, other living beings, how the world operates, and her role in being a compassionate conduit for improving life for all. Every act in social spirituality should come from compassion—at least, that is the intention.

Sikhism is extremely strong in this path of giving and service to society. It also includes community work that makes seekers more aware of the world's problems and gives them an opportunity to contribute meaningfully to improve the world around them. Every major religion, and every big and small corporate, has some form of giving and sharing built into its philosophy. The aim is to understand ourselves as part of the larger system and not separate from it.

In yoga, this form of service is called karma yoga, the path of rightful action in which the doer offers every service with full attention and awareness but is not attached to the results of the action. The doer simply serves because it is work to be done. In the ashrams, seekers are often seen cleaning the toilets with the same attention and interest as they are seen cleaning the altar and prayer space. They are seen raking the leaves in the garden with the same interest as they are seen wiping clean the kitchen floor. The intent is to do the best job of cleaning these spaces while dissociating from the reward of it. A true karma yogi does not expect a pat on the back from anyone that the kitchen floor is shining or that the altar is so clean. She simply does the work and moves on to another job.

At the external level, social work allows us to engage proactively with our social world. In increasing this awareness of the external world, the seeker begins to notice changes in her internal world. The ego gradually dissipates with more awareness of the world outside and of others beyond the Self. In that sense, this type of spiritual work is also an internal experience. Only the route is through external, social work.

* * *

You might choose one type of spirituality as a starting point, but they all eventually converge, mix, and meld in a way that they throw light on your internal life experience. Working with the physical body, mind, or the world around 'us' is all about what is happening inside us and how we understand it.

All spiritual practices, whichever path they follow, are, ultimately, aimed at the same thing—to shed the ego, which would then enable us to switch on the inner light. Ego is a strong element that blocks the inner light from shining. All spiritual work is to trick the ego into moving out of the way or better still to eliminate it completely so that our true selves, our light, can be revealed to us and to the world.

If we consider Sergei's example, his chosen way of spirituality doesn't necessarily strictly follow any one of the types or paths. And yet, everything that he did, the life that he had designed for himself, spoke effectively to each of these pathways. He did the bodywork by being nimble and fit through movement and travel. Wherever he stayed, he found a job locally so that he had a regimen, a daily order of things to do, and a discipline that it demanded. He cared deeply for the environment, the only religion worth following (in his words). He gave and served by just being mindful of the little acts, which were highly impactful, like not littering, not disturbing the peace when in a spot of nature, and being respectful to locals everywhere he travelled. It is not one method over the other. They all coexist and work in tandem.

Similarly, while designing your personal brand of spirituality, you can find elements from different pathways to create a unique style that you can call your own. This would also keep one motivated to engage with it consistently in the long-term.

The Universal Human Experience

Many schools of spirituality, which are mostly organisations that point the torch in the direction of what they think spirituality is, rely on the concept of the universal human experience. This is nothing but becoming aware of a connection to something bigger than ourselves. Some call this a connection to God, the Source, Universal Light, Universal Life Giver, and many other names.

In pursuing a spiritual path and striving to make this connection to the Source, the interconnectedness of our inner world and outer experience cannot be ignored. The biggest questions that often drive us towards spirituality are to know: Who am I? Why am I here? Where am I going? And what are my identity and purpose?

The process of being spiritual, or rather finding answers to these questions, can grow from inside out, in which we first work on our inner self and then let that awareness expand outside. Or it can start outside and then facilitate a change within.

Our two worlds of inner and outer existence are part of the same continuous line. Any spiritual work would include any one or, ideally, both ends of this line. Some paths work from the outside and create the conditions for inner transformation to take place. The outside to inner world journey would typically be through service and community work triggering an inner positive shift. Some other paths prefer to start within by finding ways to control the Self.

The internal to external through line, and vice versa, is necessary to complete the spiritual journey. The inner light has to shine through in every aspect of your life. Until this happens, the work is not done. Extreme focus on the internal spiritual experience while having little to no awareness about the external world almost renders the internal work useless. This dissonance causes other problems, too, because the strength of the inner work is being misused by people on the outside.

The Internal and External Experiences

Saraswati, an 87-year-old neighbour, is one such example. Her devotion and hours spent on daily prayer is on full display every morning. I hear the prayer bells from her temple inside the house. She diligently washes the doorstep of her home and stands in front of the house, eyes closed in a trance-like state, chanting mantras with a fervent plea to the powers beyond this world. Her body language suggests complete surrender and total love for the gods that she calls upon every day.

Saraswati walks with a gentle grace, as though she is gliding slightly above the ground. Her movements are almost angelic. But her piercing eyes observe everything and her mind makes notes, ticking with agility about what serves her purpose and what does not.

The scent of devotion wafts through Saraswati's house in flavours of sandalwood, jasmine, rose, and other woody smells. The sounds of devotional chants are always being played in the background. When I first visited her house, she took me to her prayer room and proudly showed off the pure-silver *mandap*, the ornately decorated stage on which the Hindu idols sat. It would have cost a big fortune to have that made, and Saraswati was proud of it. I thought I saw silvery rays of light in her twinkling eyes when she flailed her hands in the direction of the mandap to flaunt its beauty.

For Saraswati, the mandap was the ultimate symbol of her devotion. She sat for hours before this silver mandap, chanting mantras, performing rituals, and feeding her internal spiritual world. But what happened the moment she stepped out of her prayer room? Saraswati switched into a terrifying matriarch that controls all that she surveys.

The power of money afforded her a troop of servants at her beck and call. Saraswati doled out instructions to them, often rudely calling them dimwits and nincompoops. She had set ways in which she wanted the household to run and made sure that her house help stretched their muscle and time to please her. She did this with not just her own hired help but with anyone who worked at the service level around her.

The building's security guard told me, 'She once asked me to flip a mattress in her house and tried to offer me Rs 2. I told her to keep it.' In many ways, Saraswati was stuck in the 1950s when she, perhaps, first started to run a household unsupervised.

The security guard now runs away at the sight of her and hides behind the garden plants, pretending to not hear her when she calls out to him. This is the case with most of the house help surrounding Saraswati today. The honest and truly reliable help refuse to work around her, and the ones that do work with her use Saraswati's limited knowledge of the new ways of the world to fleece her. The grapevine has it that she has been swindled of lakhs of rupees with the maids having the last laugh as Saraswati carries on with the illusion that she is the one in control.

The old woman's extreme arrogance stemming from material wealth has wreaked havoc in all her relationships, too. Family members that live only a few kilometres away barely visit her. If she meets someone new, Saraswati is constantly thinking of ways to use this person for her benefit. Saraswati's story speaks to the fault lines that most of us carry about equating devout people to kind people as though being God-fearing erases our other responsibilities as humans. When new people meet her and the illusion of her kindness shatters, people naturally tend to move away, leaving Saraswati to be only surrounded by those who also seek some kind of profit from her as she does from them. It becomes a mutually self-serving exchange.

But this kind of a benefit-oriented social life leads to many problems. Saraswati's loneliness pierces through the concrete walls. Her silent screams for attention go unheard and, pushed to a corner, her adamant behaviours become even more adamant. Invigorated by her religious work, she holds on steadfastly to her beliefs and ego, deeming it to be right. It's a useless situation that achieves nothing.

Why is this happening to Saraswati when she is so religious, feeding her internal life with devotion? The problem is that the awareness that she is generating while sitting in front of her silver mandap and chanting for hours is not carrying through to her day. She has created a separation of God's work from every other work. The chain of her spiritual work is breaking the moment she physically steps out of her prayer room. Her internal work is feeding her with the power of intuition but she is leaving it behind in her spiritual space while crossing a symbolic border to the material workings of the day.

The absence of this through line renders useless all the strength gained from her spiritual work. Saraswati is using that strength to posture power and a false sense of control through the lens of material wealth. There is devotional work but no psychological practise or social awareness.

Her experiences with people betray a desire for control and one-upmanship rather than allowing the inner light to lead the way. When the internal spiritual experience is rich but the outer experience is starved, it is an indication that more awareness needs to be created for a seamless flow of the benefits to be had from the tough spiritual work. Reflection and introspection do wonders to achieve this, but in most cases, simply observing our surroundings reveal much about the gaps that prevent the internal-to-external flow.

While Saraswati's story speaks to the fault lines of internal-to-external experiences, the opposite case of external-to-internal through line is equally important. Take the examples of actor Robin Williams and media personality Anthony Bourdain from recent years. They displayed happy, extroverted, and engaged lives but couldn't carry the burden of their internal life, its thoughts, drama, and torture, and decided to end the agony by taking their own life.

Closer home, I know many people around me who escape their internal voices by drowning in the din of other people's problems and lives. Such people come as messiahs to help their friends, elevating social experiences above all else but do little for their own spiritual growth. There is a faulty posturing of selflessness here, in which those of us who focus more on the external relationships seek to stay in its safe cocoon.

'I have only flirted along the fringes of spirituality but never had the courage to really look within,' a friend confessed to me. She is the kindest, most helpful woman I know but is too afraid to introspect on her journey. Her inner light is reflecting outward brilliantly but is not trained inward where she can see what truly lies within.

A well-rounded, spiritual experience can only be had when the inner light shines through end-to-end. This is a difficult process, one that demands constant work, increased awareness, practise, and loads of patience.

Is Spirituality the Concept of Trying to 'Fix' Oneself?

'Fix' is an inappropriate word. A better word would be 'improve' or 'refine'. Fixing something would imply that it is broken. And one of the ideas that any spiritual path teaches is to accept ourselves the way we are. While we are already perfect, there is always room for improvement, and this desire to be better triggers change.

Any change is uncomfortable, hence the resistance, especially if it questions our long-held beliefs about life. It is the work of spirituality to peel the layers of resistance and unwanted fat sitting within us in the form of negative emotions. Once these layers are peeled, we find our true selves beneath it all. That's when the light comes on, and we can see clearly.

This idea of fixing the self is hidden in the bias that spirituality is only for those who go through bad times or have hit a dead end with their problems. But spirituality is for everyone. Everyone can do with some improvement. If our inner light is not switched on, we can start there. If our inner light is on but dim, we can work on making it brighter. If our inner light is already shining, we can make it burn brighter to reach more people. If our inner light is glowing to perfection, it is time to help others with the process of switching on their inner light.

Sergei let his inner light shine bright by leading through example. His gentle actions and behaviours of poise, while being calm and sprightly, too, was a role model on letting the inner light take the lead.

And that is what spirituality is all about.

3

Exploring Spirituality

'Stop searching the world for treasure, the real treasure is in yourself.'

—Pablo Picasso

MY PARENTS ARE RITUALISTICALLY RELIGIOUS. IN MY ancestral home, where I grew up, every Hindu festival was celebrated as per traditional customs. My mother would prepare the specific sweet dish to appease the God to be welcomed home on that day. The prayer room would be cleaned and decorated. I would wear shiny, silk clothes and arrange flowers in my hair.

My early exposure to religion was strong, which left a deep impression on my mind. I didn't think of any ritual as esoteric, whether it was the incantations for the various gods or the belief that their spirit truly resides in the idols that we worshipped. Beliefs like these would generally require a huge leap of faith. For me, as for most of us growing up in a religious household, the practice of believing was ingrained since childhood. I truly believed that religious rituals all worked as I trusted that they should. To my understanding, as I have mentioned earlier, religion and spirituality were synonymous, both to do with mysticism.

It was only in my teens that I began to understand the difference between religion and spirituality when I saw my father bringing home books on meditation, energy work, *kundalini shakti* (serpent power), tantra, and yoga. He was at that stage in his midlife when he was devouring books on spirituality with an aim of finding the meaning and purpose of life. I tried reading some of these books but they didn't make any sense to me, so, I gave up quickly.

One afternoon, when I was bored and home alone, I picked up a copy of *Brida* by Paulo Coelho and opened the book to a random page and started reading. The page had an exercise to test your own power of inner knowing and seeing. The exercise asked you to sit comfortably, calm the mind through some deep breathing, and allow the mind to travel out of your body, out of the room, out of the house, and out on to the main street. The aim of the exercise was to allow the mind to travel to a shop near your house, preferably, an apparel store, observe the display window, and notice what the mannequins were wearing. Then make the mind travel back the same route it went, and return to where you were sitting.

I thought of the exercise as some woo-woo nonsense at first. There was no way you could see what was happening at another place just through your mind's eye. But because I was so bored, I decided to give it a try, absolutely sure that it was not going to work. Although I didn't believe in the exercise, I did it in all honesty.

I sat on my bed, cross-legged, and allowed my mind to fly out the door. I looked at all the neighbours' houses, noticed their gates and front yards, the colour of their homes, and the plants growing around the houses. I took the turn to the main street behind my house and stopped in front of a branded apparel shop. I noticed a hat on one mannequin, a shiny silver top on another one, and white shorts on a seated mannequin staring back at me. The mannequins were all dressed in the theme of white.

My mind returned the same way, taking the same turns and back to my body. I opened my eyes and smiled. I would now walk that way to the store and check the shop window to see what was on display. I walked out the main door of my house and noticed the neighbouring houses, their windows and doors, the colours, and plants. I turned to the main street towards the store and stood in my tracks. I was shocked to see all the mannequins dressed in white exactly as I had imagined in my mind's eye only a few minutes ago in my bedroom.

I stood transfixed, staring impossibly at the store display for a long time. Then, I walked home slowly, in a stupor of disbelief. What was that? I wondered. My curiosity was at its peak. I picked up the book and read it without a break to find answers. It wasn't sufficient. In the next few days, I hungrily read all of Paulo Coelho's books, one after the other, in quick succession hoping to find out how was it possible that I could see the window display exactly as it was without first physically seeing it with my own eyes. I couldn't find any satisfactory answers to my initial question about the display window, but all that reading opened my mind to new ideas and thoughts about the vast subject of spirituality in a way that I had never before understood. From here, there was no turning back.

Where to Start the Exploration

I had found a trigger in an exercise that I had chanced upon in a book. But even before that, I had been aware of the spiritual world when I had overheard family members discuss certain concepts and teachings in this space, although it was only years later that my own practice took off. But there are many among us who may not have had any triggers and still would like to take those first steps into learning more about spirituality to bring balance and a more holistic approach to living. Where do we then start this exploration?

The initial spiritual exploration can be categorised into three large buckets:

- **Books and online videos**

  These are largely self-directed, based on the online search world. They could also come through friend recommendations.

- **Religion**

  Religion is a natural entry point for the exploration of spirituality. This entails going deeper into studying the religious practices that one already understands reasonably well. There is a familiarity that one builds upon to go deeper into practices and find a path that one wants to explore further.

- **Healing-led philosophies and practices**

  These would be centred on philosophies at the heart of which are healing practices like reiki, pranic healing, sound healing, or crystal-healing therapies. The exploration of these could be triggered by the need for self-healing or through friendly recommendations.

Books Are a Wealth of Information

Whether there is an external trigger to pay attention to spirituality or as a self-motivated exercise for expanding awareness, a good place to start learning more would be to read books on this topic. Books are, unarguably, a great source of knowledge and information on any subject. Spirituality is no different.

The next question, then, would be: Which book do I start with? It's best to start with the most popular books of writers and teachers that you may have already come across. Unless you read those books, it would be difficult to form your personal opinion on them. So, start somewhere. Pick a book and start reading. If you have absolutely no idea where to begin, then do an internet search for the top 10 spiritual books for beginners. From this list, pick a book and get started.

If you are not much into reading and would rather engage with audiovisual aids, then the best thing to do is to watch videos. Here, again, start with a question you may have, such as 'what is spirituality?' and see what comes up. Does the video answer your questions? Then, start your exploration by watching other videos on similar subjects. This will broaden your mind and provide you with a greater knowledge on the subject.

The most important thing to bear in mind while exploring different ideas and concepts of spirituality is to keep an open mind. You could come across wildly differing points of view on the same topic. If you read the celebrated leadership expert Robin Sharma of the *The Monk Who Sold His Ferrari* fame, you will come across his emphasis on the future. Sharma urges his readers to spend more time designing their future. 'Less Past, More Future. Stop being a prisoner of your past. Become the architect of your future,' he writes. But if you read Indian mystic and Guru Osho, his teachings are focused on bringing us back from the past and the future to the present moment. 'And the only way to live, love, enjoy, is to forget the future. It exists not,' he says in *The Book of Wisdom: The Heart of Tibetan Buddhism*. Even the spiritual teacher Deepak Chopra offers meditation courses on practising living in the present moment.

Try to hold space for these different ideas. Remember that much of what is expressed in books by spiritual seekers is their own experience. Treat it as such—the story of a spiritual seeker and what she encountered along her journey. But every journey is assuredly different from another's. This uniqueness is the only thing that is certain in the spiritual world.

An expectation that your journey should be similar to one that you read about is setting you up for disappointment. Your journey could be somewhat similar but, in most cases, it isn't. It's best to treat the exploration phase as watching several movies on the same subject but written by different scriptwriters and directors with their unique vision for film-making. Just as any creative expression is neither right nor wrong, every kind of spiritual path also has its rightful place in the sun.

Religion as a Base

Religion is a naturally good fit to get deeper into spiritual exploration. To use an analogy, religion is akin to an aircraft taxiing on the runway, while spirituality is the actual take-off and cruising at high altitudes. One can start with study of the most popular religious texts. There are numerous abridged versions and easy-to-understand, practical interpretations of the famous religious texts available today. What's more, there are online courses on deeper understanding of these texts, too, but this could come at the next level. An initial exploration through self-reading would be the first step to figuring out if one wants to go deeper into this study.

Mythology, which in many parts of the world has become a part of religion, also offers insights into the spiritual dimension. The beauty of understanding spirituality through religious mythology is that the messages are wrapped in glorious tales of yore. In most mythological narratives, fantasy meets morality meets spirituality. These stories are easily accessible, and one can take a pick from a wide range of fascinating stories from Hindu, Nordic, and Greek mythology and more.

While pursuing spiritual exploration through religion, a common problem that one could face would be in finding teachers who exhibit a balanced view of religious teachings. Religious teachers are often great experts of their own field of study. This is good if you have chosen this path and wish to go deeper. What can be a killjoy for beginners in the learning process is a teacher's strict adherence to one viewpoint while shunning debate and discussion. Be aware of this while choosing teachers, and prepare your mind on what to expect from them.

Healing and Spirituality

The third way of exploration is through energy work-led healing practices. My own path started in this way and organically expanded to the first two. I stumbled upon a tarot card teacher and began my journey into the esoteric space by learning how to read tarot cards. Then, I met a reiki teacher who attuned me to the first degree of reiki healing. In a way, I didn't go seeking these practices. They came my way, and I was open to learning them. Moreover, I was loyal to my practice and continued engaging with them for years; I still continue to do so.

It requires making spirituality an integral part of your lifestyle. It is not separate from you. And you make time for it as you make time for other aspects of your life like health, career, hobbies, and relationships. So, the choice of spiritual paths to explore should be one where you are willing to make a commitment for a long-term relationship. But it should, in no way, be a daunting or scary affair. One wouldn't know unless one tried a path. So, go at it with an open mind of learning and exploration.

This demands both discipline and consistency. It was only after the first three years of consistent practice that I was beginning to understand some of how the world of energy and spirituality works. I dug deeper and then started to choose practices that I was naturally drawn to. To my repertoire of learning, I then added Vedanta, shamanism, crystal healing, yoga, and Vedic astrology. These happened gradually, over a span of 20 years. But I consider my roots to be in reiki healing practices. And from here, every form of learning has only further added to my understanding of the world of energy and spirituality.

In that sense, my exploration and choice were both natural and linear, in which I stuck to one form of practice for several years before expanding to others. The search has been organic, gradual, and inclusive to my larger path.

Stop the Endless Snacking

The next question that could come to mind is: How long should the period of exploration last? The initial search should ideally last till one has zeroed in on 2–3 paths or teachers or studies that one is interested to delve deeper into. This could take some of us weeks or months of steady work—with, at least, 3–5 hours of investment per week—and, typically, should end in a few months and no longer.

It would help to give oneself a deadline and stop the exploration phase because it is tempting to go on and on, snacking endlessly on bite-sized information and ideas without really getting deeper into the practice. There are many self-taught seekers who get stuck at this stage of exploration for decades, often mistaking the exploration itself for the learning. The years of reading and self-learning, no doubt, gives them a wide lens through which they understand spirituality. They are even able to hold forth on debates about the different paths and practices. But their own personal practice could be lacking in discipline. For there are many advantages for the seeker from prolonged exposure to one type of practice and dedication.

There is benefit to be had from sacrificing creativity for the rigor of daily practice. Compared to this dreary, everyday exercise, the idea of continued creative searching sounds far more inviting. The constant exploration of new ideas stimulates the mind and feeds it new information on a daily basis. It's so much like a shot of adrenaline, one that is too easy to get addicted to.

But once you stop floating and narrow down 2–3 paths to drop anchor and explore in depth, you will be doing the same practice daily and getting into the rhythm. Zeroing in on the paths to deep dive into isn't, by any measure, a final decision, nor is it nonreversible. But it is important as it lends structure to the study, helping one to focus without distraction while learning about everything that one path has to offer.

How to Pick the Paths to Explore First?

In the process of exploration, there are paths that simply call out to you more than the others. There are those ideas that one feels naturally inclined to follow. They could also be the ones that trigger your curiosity. These seem like a natural fit and are the ones that should make at the top of your list.

Whichever path you choose should leave scope for gathering knowledge, exploring your inner life, and the actual practice. In all, it should be a well-balanced path. If you are drawn to 2–3 paths, which are to be expected in the exploration stage, then find definitive structures from which to study them.

Not a Linear Path

There is no linear path to start this exploration from because, unlike learning a technical subject, one's engagement with spirituality is bound to be at a deeply personalised, experiential level. So, a person who may never have read a single book on spirituality, nor had a discussion on any of the concepts with anyone may find the beginner books too simple, and they could be ready for advanced practices. At the same time, a person who has read beginners' books for decades may need to continue doing so for some more time. These levels are not linear in time and space. It doesn't mean that a person who is ready for advanced level practices is superior or better off. It just means that she is walking along her individual spiritual path and, to get to her destination, this is her personal pace and learning level.

It is also quite possible that in the very initial stages, you could be completely repulsed by one school of thought. Maybe, it didn't meet your expectations, or it just wasn't the kind of study that you wanted to undertake. It is fine to let it go and move on to another path that seems like a better fit for your personal journey.

This happened to me once many years ago when a friend recommended—actually forced me to sign up for—a healing workshop. I paid up for the two-day workshop, and on the morning of the first day, in the very first class, I didn't want to continue. I couldn't pinpoint why I felt that way, but it was a strong intuition that I needed to leave. I didn't want to be rude to the teacher and my fellow classmates. So, I managed to sit through the entire first day, and then decided to not continue the workshop.

What followed was a barrage of calls and messages from the organisation for me to attend the second day and, at one point, it was a veiled threat. The organisation seemed too obsessed with their work for me to be comfortable to continue the study in that environment. I knew that I had made the right decision to leave. But this isn't at all to say that there is anything wrong with that modality or even the organisation. There were ten others in my class and they all seemed perfectly happy with their study. It just didn't feel like a good fit for me, which is okay. It is also important to honour how one feels about these things. Spiritual work is a deeply personal experience and it demands high levels of honesty with the Self. This is also part of the self-healing process—one we should acknowledge.

Pitfalls to Avoid during the Spiritual Exploration Phase

- **Overwhelm from the influx of information**
  As you start the exploration into various spiritual paths, you are bound to be bombarded by numerous schools and organisations. New ones are cropping up every single day. Many of these paths are packaged attractively and you will feel like trying them all out. But there have to be certain parameters that you follow in your search. The very first and obvious parameter is that you feel naturally attracted towards that school of thought or teacher. You don't need to explain to anyone else why you feel so, but it is

important that you are honest with yourself about feeling inclined towards a path or not liking it. Some paths are led by individual gurus. Entire organisations, corporations, and empires are built around that one guru. Take, for instance, Baba Ramdev or Sadhguru or Mata Amritanandamayi or Sri Sri Ravi Shankar. They run global organisations and millions around the world have resonated with their teachings. Then there are paths led by religion. These, too, have sects and groups, sometimes, led by a guru—for example, the Sringeri Mutt in South India led by one chosen guru.

But there are also many teachers who simply impart the insights from a sacred text. For example, there are teachers who specialise in teaching how to chant the Bhagavad Gita. Iskcon, another global organisation, is dedicated to the teaching of the Gita. Then there are also schools of philosophy that teach many different paths in one place by offering various courses. An example could be the Sivananda Yoga Vedanta Centres, New Acropolis School of New Age Philosophy, or The Shift Network online, etc. So, whether it is guru-led, religion-led, or philosophy-led, test your natural inclination and choose what feels right to you. The pitfall to avoid is feeling overwhelmed by information excess, leading you to self-sabotage the process at the very beginning of the exploration and then giving up.

- **Comparing peer influences and experiences**

Unless working one-on-one with a teacher, you will likely meet like-minded seekers and form connections with them in class and outside. This can be a huge benefit to learning, in which the peer sharing of information can open up new pathways and opportunities for learning. It also opens up the mind to exploring paths that one hadn't earlier encountered in the exploration stage. The benefit of peer learning and influence can be a huge gift to the journey. Even with peer interactions, there is bound to be excessive information exchange. The pitfall to avoid here is to compare peer experiences to your own and then judge whether you are slow or fast, good or bad on your journey. It becomes necessary to constantly remind the Self that every individual experience is her own, and this is not a race. It is a personal journey with individual goals and unique destinations.

- **The trap of superlatives and jargon**

  The spiritual world has the reputation for being arcane, mysterious, and filled with complicated concepts. But it needn't be. If, as a beginner, a teacher's message isn't making sense or reaching out to your general level of understanding, don't be afraid to move on. Many seekers start out believing that they need to struggle with the jargon and that's part of the process. Not necessarily! If a teacher isn't reaching your level of perception, then change the teacher. Similarly, if peers seem to be using jargon, don't be overwhelmed. For example, there is a Facebook group in which people discuss ascension symptoms—physical aches, pains, and pressures that they believe are symptoms that they are ascending to the next spiritual dimension. The concept itself is hard to grasp. On top of it, the group's members share all kinds of information on the earth's electromagnetic signals and other information that is difficult to understand. It is important that the seeker not be overwhelmed by this overload of information, and instead keeps moving along her individual path while exploring other ideas and concepts.

- **Extreme love for one path; resistance to another path**

  Often, the first love is said to be the best and most favourite. And I don't deny my partiality towards tarot cards as it was the one that opened me up to new ways of understanding the world. Even more than a decade later, I go back to tarot cards for meditation, introspection, and comfort and solace. But had I adamantly stuck to tarot cards, refusing to open up to any other modality, I would not have gained access to all the beautiful knowledge that is available out there. At the exploration stage, it is important to keep an open mind about several different modalities as they all have a place in the spiritual world and have benefited people in one way or another. While it is essential to not take love for one path to an excessive degree, it is also important to try and not resist a path so much that the benefits from that path are blocked. Bear in mind that resistance is also, at times, a sign that you, perhaps, need to push through a persistent block in your life. Try to keep the middle ground with no extreme opinions on anything. Just as people and relationships are transient, and only the memories stay, spiritual paths run along parallel tracks but lead to the same destination of self-realisation. It's good to be relaxed and casual while not too hung up on this path or that guru. This neutral attitude can bring the maximum benefit to your explorations.

- **The desire to know too much too soon**

  Spirituality is a slow process; one that takes a lifetime of practice. Actually, even one lifetime isn't enough. Once a seeker has developed an initial taste for it and experienced the benefits, there is a growing desire to want more and more. It's a lot like eating ice cream—it is to be savoured slowly and gradually; with each bite, the flavours explode in the mouth and the chill pervades the senses. But if had too soon, in one big gulp, the ice cream feels too cold. Besides, the chill numbs out the senses, preventing us from experiencing the taste, texture, flavour, and temperature as it was originally made to enjoy. Spirituality is quite similar. Once a seeker hits upon a guru, a spiritual path, or an idea that resonates with her, the temptation is to dive in too deep too quickly. Taking that big gulp could lead to indigestion or, worse, ill health. Spiritual lessons must be paced slowly, for their learning is to be experienced through your daily life and happenings around you, something that cannot be rushed. When I first read *Brida* and went through the inner knowing exercise, I was overcome with the desire to know too much too soon. I read so many books so quickly that I didn't really take in their lessons as they were meant to be understood. It became a

> purely intellectual experience. So, after many years, I had to reread the books to do them justice. When I sat with these books again, I understood them better and in a different light. I was not in a hurry to get anywhere. And that made all the difference.

That first step on the spiritual journey is important because it opens uncountable doors and possibilities. Of course, we are free to jump on parallel paths and go back and forth, as we should in our explorations. However, the first step will always be remembered as special.

4

How to Start Meditating

'Feelings come and go like clouds in a windy sky.
Conscious breathing is my anchor.'
—Thich Nhat Hanh

THE OFFICE HALL WAS REVERBERATING WITH PEALS of laughter as my co-workers huddled around Sachin, poking fun at his loud snoring during the meditation retreat the previous day. All employees were compulsorily made to go to a retreat for stress relief, which Sachin had attended along with several others.

Sachin was an overstressed and overweight field reporter who moved through the city traffic and noise every day to bring the best news together. At the meditation retreat, which involved hours of silence and quiet contemplation, Sachin had promptly fallen asleep at every meditation session and had begun snoring loud enough for his intermittent snores to pierce through the silence of the meditation hall.

The retreat assistants had tapped on his shoulders, tugged at his big toe, and whispered into his ear to gently wake him up. Sachin would wake up with a start, and then again promptly return to sleep.

Sachin may not have been able to meditate during the session but he got some much-needed sleep. His body craved rest, and in the calming environment of the retreat, he was able to quieten his body and mind.

Years later, Sachin had voluntarily retired from the stressful day job and had made time to learn meditation and yoga. He was now a regular, and I almost didn't recognise him when I bumped into him at a restaurant when he was gorging on masala dosa and coffee. The cloud of anxiety had cleared from his face, and he smiled more often. Between mouthfuls of masala dosa, he told me that he was enjoying his early retirement and now made time for many hobbies, including trekking, and he even was a meditation teacher.

'Obviously, you're not snoring anymore while meditating,' I giggled, recalling his time at the retreat a few years ago.

'Of course, not. But many of my students do. And I let them snore,' he laughed along.

First Stop Is Meditation

Once you have decided that spirituality needs some of your attention, what next?

Ask anyone about taking the first baby steps into spirituality, and they will tell you to meditate. Troubled? Meditate. Anxious? Meditate. Confused? Meditate. Sad? Meditate. Hungry? Meditate. Okay, maybe, first get some food. But you get the drift.

Meditation is almost synonymous with spirituality, and for good reason. Spiritual seekers at all levels of working with their inner light first practise meditation. It is a time-tested relaxation technique. It is believed to get you in touch with your intuition and improve its functioning. Meditation is also preparation for deeper inner work.

Where Does One Start with Meditation?

There are different types of meditation. It is not possible to pin down the number of types or all of its definitions, which often overlap. But as a beginner explores this world of meditation, she could come across some names. It is important to not be overwhelmed. But for your information, and just so you are familiar with these names when you stumble upon them, here are a few.

There are two broad types of meditation: Concentrative meditation and mindfulness meditation. In concentrative meditation, the practitioner focuses on a point or an object of concentration, commonly one's own breath or a mantra or a light and stay focused on that point for the entire period of meditation. Mindfulness meditation is more about expanding awareness to specific issues. The issues that one meditates on could change during every session. The aim is to become more open, aware, and accepting of the issues, and, at a deeper level, also, perhaps, let go of unwanted emotions related to a particular difficulty.

There are many more types of meditation like kundalini, Zen, chakra, yoga nidra, raja yoga, transcendental, vipassana, loving-kindness, breath awareness, I am, qigong, Taoist, and so many more. It takes a lifetime of work and dedication to learn these different techniques. But it is important to be aware that these are all but different pathways to the same ultimate goal of switching on your inner light, working with your inner light, and allowing your inner light to heal you and the world around you.

To that end, it is quite unnecessary to stress over which type of meditation to choose and which one is better. Instead of spending time on researching these types and ending up nowhere, it is better to dive in and start on any one type. But better than immediately joining a class in enthusiasm and not being regular—much like most of our gym visits and short-lived New Year resolutions—it is better to do some initial personal work.

Try Sample Online Videos

As a start to get familiar with meditation and what it could feel like, just scour the many online videos that come up when you search for 'guided meditation'.

They all have soothing music, a calming image from nature like the mountains or the beach, and a soft voice guiding you to focus on the breath or on an object of concentration. Bear in mind that it may take you a few days of searching to hit upon a guided meditation that truly resonates with you. There are some videos in which you may not like the voice—it might be too deep, too squeaky, or too distracting for you. There could be other videos in which you feel that the sound of rushing water is making you want to go to the bathroom. There could be some videos that don't optimise the short time and instead use most of it in giving instructions on when to meditate, where to sit, how to sit, etc. These instructions are important, but after the first few times of hearing them, you will want to get straight to the practice. Be patient as you check out different videos till you find the one that best suits your need.

There are so many options out there that it is simply not possible that you will not find even one that resonates with your sensibility. You could stumble upon this perfect, guided practice at the very first instance or it could take a few tries and misses before you manage to find it. But you will. And remember that this is only the start of the process. The purpose of the online video is more like a teaser for you to imbibe a long-term relationship with meditation.

Start with a five-minute guided meditation and test your own concentration level and ability to sit still for those five minutes and do as instructed.

When you sample a few different forms of meditation out there, you will come across various methods and processes. Some schools of meditation work purely with breath, while some others work with an object or a point of concentration. Whatever the tools and the methodology, the aim of all meditation is the same—to make the mind stop with the chatter and quiet down for a bit. Make meditation your weapon against the non-stop prattle in your head.

No Two Days Are the Same

Every time you meditate, you go on an inner journey that is a uniquely creative expression of your experience. Every person's spiritual journey is different. Not just that, every meditation session for each practitioner also differs from day-to-day. My meditation experience from yesterday will never be the same as my experience from today. And I can be sure that tomorrow will be something different, too.

This is because each of us is changing every moment. I am not the same person that I was yesterday. The experience of meditation gets us in touch with our changing nature so that we don't travel so far out that we lose track of who we are anymore. In that sense, the purpose of meditation is to bring us back to our inner light, reintroduce us to it, and to work with it.

It is not unusual to experience very different meditations on most days despite following the same technique at the same time in the same environment every day.

It is also not prudent to expect the same calm that you experienced on one day to continue every day. One day could be peaceful and the next could bring up some uncomfortable anxieties, and the one after that could make you angry. These highs and dips are certainly not a sign that the meditation isn't working. In fact, your consistency with the practice will reveal many insights about the inner workings of the mind, which is all the more reason to stay with the practice no matter what emotions it brings up.

Maintain a Meditation Journal

For a beginner, it is a great idea to track any changes in emotions and mental relaxation when you meditate. The entries in the meditation journal need not be too elaborate. It could be a simple temperature check on how you feel. It needn't relate to your experience from the previous day either. Write each journal entry about how you felt at the end of that day's session.

When you have tracked your emotions for about a month, review your notes to find patterns and deeper insights about how far you have come. The longer you maintain the tracker, the more you will understand your evolving relationship with meditation.

The changes in one's life due to regular meditation practice have a long-lasting, deep effect. This is the reason it is prescribed as a general tonic for everyone, irrespective of the level of their spiritual understanding. And what a great tonic it is! Whether the Dalai Lama or a newbie to spiritual work, everyone meditates to keep their inner light glowing.

How Long Should One Ideally Sit to Meditate?

There are varying ideas about this, too. Some schools of thought believe that you must sit in meditation for the same number of minutes as your age. So, a 10-year-old would sit for 10 minutes and a 45-year-old would sit for 45 minutes.

There are other schools of thought that insist on a minimum 30-minute, daily meditation. The belief is that without, at least, this much time one does not get the benefit of meditation at all. There are other schools that lay the foundation for practitioners to sit for longer and longer hours. For example, there is the Buddhist Theravada tradition of vipassana meditation, which is a course of deep inner work done under professional guidance in which the participant would sit for 8–10 hours a day, or more, in meditation. This technique focuses on the disciplined attention to the body's physical sensations. It makes one pay attention to the body's needs and to learn to listen to them deeply. This experience is often intense and brings powerful results as well.

What is important is that you start at a time investment that is most practical for you. It is better to meditate for five minutes every day rather than not meditate at all for weeks because you could not take out 30 minutes from your day.

When you look online, or at the zillions of apps available, you will find meditations ranging from one minute to one hour, and more. Start with a one-minute calming meditation or a five-minute practice. This is only to get accustomed to the idea of meditation. For those among us who are not used to sitting cross-legged on the floor, this can be good practice. We could test our own ability to shut out the world for just those few minutes. We could experiment with different corners of the house until we find the one where the dog doesn't come wagging its tail, asking for attention, or where family members need your opinion on something. These are all systems you can check until you arrive at the ideal time and place to meditate. Once you have this figured out, freeze on it and don't change it.

It is advisable to sit at the same place and at the same time every day to meditate. The reasons are quite straightforward. It is a habit-creation tool. When you make a habit of sitting at the same place at the same time to still your mind every day, your body and your subconscious mind, too, begin to expect that behaviour and even support you to continue the practice daily. Within a few days, it won't seem that difficult anymore. Then, it would be possible to increase the time you sit to meditate.

Regarding the time of meditation, the general rule is that any time is a good time to meditate. But here again, use your discretion. It is always better to sit when you can willingly focus and concentrate on yourself for those few minutes. When you have had a large meal, the body's digestive system is overactive while the other bodily faculties seek rest. Similarly, if you are rushing against a work deadline, it goes without saying that it would be difficult to focus when your mind is on meeting the deadline. Due to these reasons, it is common practice to encourage meditation early in the morning when your mind is fresh and you can do your practice before the day takes over. Also, morning meditation sets you up with a calm state of mind to tackle the day. This could, of course, be different for some people. Some may like to meditate at night before sleeping. Yoga nidra and progressive muscle relaxation techniques are great to practice before going to bed. You need to find the time and place that best suit you. And it could also be that with different seasons of your life and varying schedules, your preferred time for meditation could change. Be flexible and go with the flow while trying to be consistent.

Books on Meditation

As mentioned above, online videos are a great start. But so are books. The self-help bookshelves across the world are overflowing with titles on how to meditate. If you fancy any of these, pick them up for your reading pleasure and to pocket some useful tips. But always bear in mind that you cannot learn how to meditate by reading a book. You can only learn how to meditate by, well, meditating.

The book could teach you a technique that you could practice, but it is your own practice that matters most. Learning how to meditate is quite similar to the idea of learning how to sleep.

Can you learn how to sleep by reading a book? The book, at best, would share statistical information on sleep disorders and wax eloquent on the best practices to improve sleep quality. It would also talk about the benefits of a good night's sleep on health, relationships, and life in general.

The book could contain information and ideas on the best mattress for quality sleep and how to create the perfect ambience in the bedroom. It could share studies on which scents induce slumber and what colours promote better sleep. But can it tell you how to actually sleep? No. You just sleep. Similarly, with meditation.

There are several books out there that share techniques for meditation—how to set up your meditation space, when is the best time of day to meditate, how to sit, where to sit, how to breathe, when to inhale, how many seconds to hold your breath, how to bring the mind back to the breath, and so on. You could gather information on these techniques from a book but the only thing that will matter is that you actually sit down to meditate.

A Cautionary Note about Recommendations

Friends and acquaintances could recommend books and meditation schools and videos that best worked for them. Their recommendations are often enthusiastic and, perhaps, with good reason because they found much peace and life purpose after they started their meditation practice. So, their recommendation to you is in good faith that you, too, find the benefit that they did.

It could happen that your trigger to learn meditation is a friend's account of how her life changed dramatically after she started meditation with this teacher or that school. If you feel enthusiastic to try it out for yourself, go ahead. But keep your expectations realistic. Your friend's experience and your experience could be extremely different. No doubt, you both have had the same external environment and the same technique taught to you. But meditation is hardly like learning how to solve a math problem. It is not formula-driven. Nor does it have a specific quantifiable end goal. The qualitative goal, of course, is that the practice brings you more and more peace. What constitutes peace differs from person to person.

It is not necessary that the meditation practice that worked for them work for you, too. Your friend is at a different time and place in her life and took to a meditation technique that worked wonders. It could do the same for you, too, but it is also possible that you need something else and a slightly different technique might work better for you. You will never know unless you try it out. Keep an open mind in your search and do not hesitate to move on from one type of practice if it isn't motivating you to sit through even for five minutes.

But does this mean that you hop like a butterfly from one technique to the next? Here's where you use your own discernment and make a choice.

When taking recommendations from friends about meditation or any spiritual practice, use cautious optimism and your better practical judgment. Assess whether you are ready to expand your personal practice or would prefer to stick to your current routine for some more time; and whether your time and resources make it a practical decision. Maybe, the meditation class is too far from your house, and, maybe, it clashes with your family time. Assess every piece of information before blindly committing to a practice out of the desire to up your meditation game or before you fall for stories of miracles and great transformations. The transformation will happen when the time is right, irrespective of where you are at that point in your life.

Learning Meditation with a Teacher

Purists may disagree with the online browsing method to get started on meditation. There are several schools of thought that insist on a teacher and a formal process of initiation into meditation, including a mantra initiation. The theory is that you exchange energy with a teacher and that divine energy flows to you.

This initiation is often insisted upon by religion-based meditation schools and spiritual organisations. The initiation could happen in one of two ways. The first is a one-on-one session with your teacher. This can be extremely valuable as you get full attention and guidance from a teacher while she shares experience notes that would be helpful for your journey.

Learning meditation with a teacher is akin to reading about the techniques of meditation from a book. The teacher, of course, could be sharing more knowledge and tips along the way, which is a huge value-add, no doubt. This, if anything, should be the more important reason to go to a teacher and to join a school.

The second way in which you could engage with a teacher could be as one in a group of students. Here, you can seek comfort in the social setting of an organisation and a homogenous group of believers. You have the opportunity to share your experiences with fellow seekers during breaks at meditation and spirituality conferences. This gives you a sense of belonging.

But it would be wise to keep in mind that the process of meditation is deeply personal. One person may have started seeing visions in her meditation, while another may see colours. But just because you see nothing does not mean that your meditation experience is any less or better than theirs. It is just different, as it should be. Remind yourself that your experience is yours alone, and it is neither inferior nor superior to anyone else's experience.

With some schools, the meditation technique is a closely guarded secret. The teaching often happens in an ashram or ashram-like setting where lifestyles and consumption for the period of stay is carefully curated. This would include healthy diet, time for exercise, rest and relaxation, and stress- and noise-free environment. When learning in an environment of like-minded, motivated fellow seekers, your journey would seem more beautiful. In such cases, aided by the setting, the meditation technique earns a curious reputation and an aura of mystery that sets it apart as almost magical.

When information is withheld, it becomes more valuable. Learn meditation from one of these schools once you have attained some level of personal discipline and practice. Here, too, keep an open mind about your expectations from the personalised teaching experience. Use your discernment on careful assessment of friends' recommendations and your own readiness for this leap.

The verdict is out on whether learning meditation directly from a teacher trumps other self-taught methods. It's about finding what eventually works best for you. And, that, nobody else but you would be best able to tell.

Shopping for a Meditation Technique

Searching for a meditation technique that fits you like a glove is much like choosing detergent. You stand at the cleaning agents' aisle in the supermarket, staring at the many brands in all forms and packaging. Some come in powder form, some in liquid, some are bars, and some others are detergent pods. They come in varying sizes and pricing, stacked from floor to ceiling. The effort to check out every single option out there can make you dizzy. But the aim of every product on that aisle is the same—to clean clothes. You eventually choose one product and check it out a few times while reviewing how your clothes smell and feel. If happy, you continue. If you feel that your clothes need some more heavy-duty cleaning or more softening, you add a softening agent along with the detergent. And so it goes.

Searching for a meditation method is similar. The aim of all kinds of meditation is to lead you to your inner light and switch it on. For a start, choose one method and try it out. See how it fits. Check out if you are able to sustain the practice. Keep at it before you review it and try another one. If there is one practice that your best friend has recommended and you feel most comfortable sticking with it, do so. But be honest with yourself about how it is working for you. Stick with it for as long as it works for you.

How Do You Know That a Meditation Is Working for You?

Each of us responds differently in the first few months of a sustained meditation practice. For some, it may bring up some uncomfortable emotions. Others could feel calmer and more aware of their environment. And another reaction could also be that you want to spend more time on it.

Whatever the change, the first thing to notice is that there is a change. How that change plays out in your life will be different from someone else's response to the same meditation technique. So, try not to compare your experience with other's. This is the reason it is wise to maintain a meditation tracker to keep notes on these changes. The ultimate goal is for you to become more still and aware of the world around you. You should ideally be pausing before responding to anything. You should be asking if what you are saying or doing is important, kind, and needed. If these things start to happen, you could be certain that the meditation practice is doing its job. Know that it doesn't mean the lack of anger or negative thoughts. These will continue to be there, as we are only human. But your awareness of the anger and negative thoughts would have increased. And this is the first step to the mastery of calm.

It could also be that there is still some more meditation to get you to these goals of stillness. Be persistent and consistent with the practice. You are meeting yourself, and you should not give up the opportunity to get to know yourself better.

Consistency and Practicality

In order to achieve and maintain consistency in your meditation practice, it is important that you choose a practice that resonates with you. Also, choose a time and place that you are comfortable with. You should be excited to get to the practice, whether it is for five minutes or 25 minutes.

A friend of mine had learned how to meditate from a teacher. The practice was a 45-minute routine that made her feel wonderful. She had only rave reviews to share about how it had changed her life. But she was unable to keep up with the practice as regularly as she would have liked. She worked in a stressful job in the airline industry with shifts at odd hours of day and night. And her meditation practice required her to do it early in the morning on an empty stomach. So often when she had to report for work at 3:00 a.m., her teacher would encourage her to wake up at 1:00 a.m. for an hour of meditation before getting ready for work. And sometimes, she would have had long working hours on the previous day. So, this practice was most impractical for her. My friend wound herself up with guilt and regret that she was unable to keep up with daily meditation.

The exacting demands of the practice that she had chosen were defeating the very purpose that it was meant for. It is necessary, therefore, to find a practice that is practical and easy to incorporate into your daily life.

The key is consistency. And if a current practice doesn't give you the flexibility to be regular, then take another look at what can be changed to bring back the consistency.

Initially, the idea of consistency sounds exciting, especially when considered from the perspective of the end results. But then the boredom of the same practice, whether meditating daily or journaling daily or practising yoga daily, can become difficult to sustain. That's when the body and mind must push through because there are many long-term benefits to be had when led by focus.

When Do You Know That You Need to up Your Game?

Upping the game could be going to 20 minutes from a 10-minute guided meditation. It could also mean trying to wake up 30 minutes earlier to meditate daily. Or it could mean including other spiritual practices like chanting or some yogic stretches in your routine.

The honest answer is that your intuition will guide you when you are ready. When you naturally feel the need to expand your personal practice, you are ready. But if you have not thought about it and are continuing with your meditation daily, that is fine, too. But do review your progress and check in with how the practice makes you feel. If you have reached a plateau where the practice is too comfortable and too familiar, it is, perhaps, time to include something more—either extend the time or challenge yourself. At any point, you should ideally keep moving forward and growing with your practice. But there are some among us who prefer to do the basic meditation required and stick with it. This is fine, too, as long as it is your intention to stay in a comfortable space with not too much of a deep exploration.

The answer to your readiness to challenge yourself lies only with you. Teachers and those with experience could offer a timeline range in terms of months or years it takes to truly imbibe a practice and own it. You may or may not choose to follow that parameter.

The only parameter that you do need to follow is that you are getting closer to your inner light; you have learned how to work with it and to feel its warmth and glow. As long as this is happening, you are on the right path.

The first step towards your inner light is to quiet the mind. When the mind is quiet, it can then hear the voices that were drowning in the din of its own incessant chatter. When the mind is quiet, it allows an expanded awareness to the things that it was too busy to notice earlier. When you begin to hear your inner voice and clarity of thought, you know that you are on the right path, and, perhaps, ready to work with your inner light.

5

The Guru and the Cult

'A teacher affects eternity; he can never tell where his influence stops.'

—Henry Adams

KUMARÉ, THE WISE PROPHET FROM INDIA, HAD BUILT a sizeable following in New Jersey in 2012. This young and stoic messenger from the gods wore orange robes, sported a long beard, and carried a mast with a trident pointing up to the sky. Expounding philosophies rooted in Indian tradition, he spoke in a broken Indian-English accent but always had sage words to share.

Most popular among his ideas was the mirror philosophy, which consisted of standing before the mirror and asking the Self questions while seeking answers from your reflection.

Kumaré's followers included Americans from different age groups and backgrounds. They all sought one thing from their new guru from India—peace of mind. One evening in 2012, after the *satsang* (a group gathering to sing devotional songs and listen to a discourse) by their guru, Kumaré made the big reveal. He told the gathering that he was neither a guru nor was he from India. He was ethnic-Indian, yes. But he was an Indian-American from New Jersey who had only visited his home country a bunch of times.

What is more is that he knew nothing about religion or spirituality. He didn't consider himself to be philosophical even. He was a young man in his early 30s who enjoyed all the material and sensual pleasures that the world capital of consumerism had to offer. Kumaré was conducting a social experiment in which he had been filming the process of creating a spiritual organisation and earning a follower base.

First, there was utter silence and disbelief to his big reveal. Then the reactions started pouring out. They were mostly mixed, ranging from violent rage to laughter as though at the end of a practical joke. Some followers walked out in a huff, leaving behind a trail of the choicest abuses for Kumaré. There were others who sat in stunned silence, unable to believe that they had dropped emotional anchor at the wrong place. There were a couple of followers who laughed it off and took it all as a joke.

This wide range of responses itself is quite telling of the types of followers that spiritual mass leaders tend to attract. Their charisma to hold the attention of every type of follower is partly what makes them public figures, aside from the spiritual knowledge that they seek to espouse, of course.

Kumaré, the fake prophet who had earned real followers, filmed his journey as a fake guru and stitched the videos together into a documentary titled *Kumaré: The True Story of a False Prophet*, which released in 2012 across the US to critical acclaim.

Why did he do this? Kumaré, whose real name was Vikram Gandhi, was overwhelmed by the blind faith in the yoga masters in the US. The then \$6-billion-a-year industry was raking in the moolah and while there was nothing wrong with that, Vikram wanted to uncloak the absurdity of what we humans believe in. The documentary was aimed to be a cautionary tale about whom we place our faith in.

So, Vikram went about creating this social experiment. How did he pull it off? First, he studied the big gurus of all time, including Jesus and Buddha. From their teachings, he made some general notes about spirituality and philosophy. Then he created his physical look. He let his hair grow long and loose, grew a beard, and started to wear orange robes like a swami. He then designed a symbol for his cult following, which was a loosely reimagined trident curved to look like buttocks—if you dared to be blasphemous.

Vikram spoke in his grandmother's Indian accent and spent a lot of alone-time with his followers, talking to them, and just being a friend. At the end of every yoga class, he always said that he was no guru, and that every person's guru is already within her or him. He was the anti-guru, a guru teaching that there is no guru. And yet, his fan base grew. His main philosophy, the exercise of standing before the mirror and talking to your reflection, was also, in an ironical way, teaching the same lesson.

During the course of this 'experiment', many of the followers reported a huge transformation, almost a life-saving grace from Kumaré, and one woman also claimed a changed DNA and a complete rewiring of her system. When the followers were beginning to invest too much emotionally in his teachings, Vikram decided to stop the exercise.

While the reactions to this social experiment ranged from anger to laughter, many followers understood, sooner or later, what Gandhi was trying to prove. How each 'devotee' reacted depended on her emotional investment in the philosophy and teachings of the guru. Those in an emotionally sensitive state of mind were likelier to get carried away in trusting the guru and in placing the burden of their happiness on him. And herein lies the root cause of the problem.

When a follower or seeker or devotee, by whichever name you call her, goes to a guru to get that high of happiness or bliss, she can be sure that it is only a temporary fix. She will want to return to the guru again and again expecting to experience the same bliss. A good guru is one who teaches you to find that state of bliss yourself, without needing another. A fine guru is one who says: 'This is how I did it. You can, too. This is the way.' And then, the guru should ideally get out of the way so that the seeker can continue on her own spiritual journey.

But some would ask: So what? I experience the state of bliss when I am around my guru. Why is that wrong? And why shouldn't I continue to seek it at the place that I know I will find it certainly?

There is nothing wrong in finding your cup of joy at the guru's satsang. Most deep spiritual work happens with the help of a teacher who shows the path and gets us started. Teachers are essential to help seekers keep a clear mind and go forth on the road ahead. Continue to seek your answers where you know you will find them.

However, what could become a problem is when this seeking becomes an addiction or blind devotion to the teacher so much so that it is detrimental to your own balance and well-being. Beginners to spirituality are often at a huge risk of this form of excessive devotion and love towards the guru to the extent that it makes the seeker unreasonable, as though she sees the world with blinkers on, and often these blinkers are provided by the guru.

Excessive emotional investment in something, anything, will open us up to vulnerability. We become dependent and ignore our own inner child hoping that another adult will take care of our emotional needs. And here is where the problem starts.

Often, the seeker runs to the guru for guidance on every small matter or needs the guru's green signal for any important decision of her life. These behaviours could go to obsessive lengths if not checked early on.

Beginners are at risk of getting too carried away with the first guru they meet. Paradoxically, one of the advantages that beginners have is to spot this tendency early on and catch it so that they remain in harmony with their material and spiritual worlds. Maintaining balance requires awareness and openness to the possibility that there could be many other pathways to reach the same goal. One need not walk on all the different pathways, but it is good to be aware that there are many roads to the one truth.

Gurus Have a Place in Society

I am not trying to paint all gurus as tricksters or frauds. Far from it. Even if a trickster, each one has a role to play in the larger scheme of things. Sometimes, it is the teacher's role to show us just how vulnerable we are. They teach us to guard our heart and emotions. Teachers give structure, guidance, and direction to one's spiritual work. They light up the road ahead so that we don't have to go in the blind and wonder if the next step could land us in a ditch or at the foothills of a mountain.

The other advantage of working with most gurus these days is the added exposure to social settings that offer solace in times of self-doubt on the largely solitary spiritual journey. The social setting of spiritual organisations has a positive influence in encouraging seekers to keep up with their practice, learn from peers, and stay motivated. Often, the spiritual calming environment created at these organisations is inviting and relieves stress while making the seeker want to return to that environment for more of that state of bliss.

While walking the path with a guru, it is wise to keep our wits about us and use our better judgment as we navigate the large, grey areas of the mind, consciousness, and other spiritual dimensions as well. In the process of spiritual initiation and deep into the work, there will be many aha moments and realisations that could change your life forever. These moments could open up a new way of understanding the world, which is the purpose of all forms of spirituality. The guru who stands by you through this process becomes part of your ecstatic experience, and it is only natural to relate the guru's role in your life to that elevated, almost supernatural, experience that she facilitated in us. This sort of awakening can be a deeply intimate experience, one from which you simply cannot separate the guru.

One also hears success stories of how a guru transformed lives. Listen to these stories with cautious optimism. Such stories and recommendations are personal experiences, but it isn't necessary that you, too, experience the same. It's rare that you are also at that same place in your life as another. The guru's teachings would have resonated with a large section of the population. Look at some of the most popular spiritual teachers in the world today. They attract millions of followers and have much energy and wisdom to share. Just like CEOs, they, too, are leaders. Remember that there are many gurus, quieter teachers, who don't shout from the mountaintops to be knowledgeable and wise.

In every way, whether it is towards a guru or a film star, it is wise to be measured in your expectation and the image that you create of that leader. Walk the balance of respect as you would pay to any other teacher . . . and the awareness that she, too, is but human.

Every one of us is a seeker. We are all just at different stages of the seeking. One may have spent her entire lifetime in spiritual pursuits while learning how to switch on the inner light. Another seeker may not have paid any attention to it but will do so at some point in life, or never at all. Just as in any field of expertise, in spirituality, too, a guru is sharing her experience of seeking.

It would be pragmatic to keep in mind that the guru too, just like us, is exactly where she is supposed to be—guiding people on the spiritual path. Understand that it is, perhaps, her life's calling to do this job of shining the light on the path for spiritual seekers. When humanised, the guru aura becomes more manageable to understand and accept. It is neither elevating her to a superhuman status nor bringing her down any level. It is only about giving context to the role of a guru in the larger scheme of things.

With this awareness instilled in you, work with the teacher with full energy and enthusiasm. When at the ashram or while working with the guru, immerse in the experience to get its maximum benefit. When there, you are completely alive in the moment; when you are out, you leave that experience behind, taking with you only the teachings that are useful to lead a peaceful life outside. When out of there, the trick is to log out completely in mind, body, and soul so that there is no room for any guru obsession to be created. This would be a good rule of thumb to apply to any relationship.

Some schools of thought believe that the line to divine realisation is traversed only and only through a guru. This keeps the guru relevant throughout the spiritual journey. Think. Why do you need an intermediary to connect with your own Source or Higher Self?

Learning a technique for meditation or rituals is one thing but once that basic learning is achieved, it is in the interest of profit-leaning spiritual organisations to create courses and packages to keep the aspirant engaged. Ask yourself if you really need it all, and confidently refuse to participate when you don't feel ready.

Trapping the Vulnerable among Us

There are many spiritual gurus in the market today from which to take your pick. Profit-led gurus create artificial needs to urgently address human emotional states like worry, conflict, emotional starvation and desire. The philosophies often carry the promise of alleviating pain, confusion and stress. For a vulnerable seeker looking for quick answers, such a promise is enticing and just what she needs. The guru's understanding of the problems, acceptance of the seeker in her vulnerable emotional state, and the promise of better times ahead are all too attractive to let pass.

Some ten years ago, my friend Sophia was in desperate need of healing from a nasty heartbreak. In her susceptible state, she searched for solutions that could take away the agony of separation. She wasn't sleeping well, nor was able to lead a peaceful life. It didn't take her long to find a retreat atop a hill in the French countryside.

The brochure for this spiritual organisation spoke directly to her heart as though the guru knew exactly what she was going through. The retreat was for those experiencing a wavering mind, lack of focus, imbalanced thoughts, desire to identify life purpose, and the need for healing. It promised to connect you to your source of life from where you can bring back your mojo. The guru was going to teach you how to tap into the unending well of happiness, so that you can always draw from the well to be joyful no matter the changing circumstances around you.

'I was so heartbroken that I would have believed anyone who could offer some semblance of peace in my life. And this guru was promising the world at my feet,' Sophia said, now reflecting on the experience from a safe emotional distance.

'It was such a beautiful hill in the French countryside. The retreat was tucked away in the back of beyond. The clouds hung low and it felt like our cottages were on the pathway to paradise. On the first morning, a bunch of forty people sat in a hall waiting for the retreat to start. We sat for some time in silence and were startled by loud music,' said Sophia.

She described it as 'grand entrance' music. Suddenly, the floor was filled with fog, artificially created, of course. The fog rose and within minutes had filled up the room. At the exact moment, the music hit a crescendo and a gust of wind blew some of the smoke outside. From the front of the room, the guru appeared.

'He was wearing an ill-fitted spanking white robe with a shawl draped over his right shoulder. He had deep-set eyes and sported a long, scraggly beard. He held up his right hand near his chest, fingers drooping loosely, like a model from a Renaissance painting,' Sophia recalled. She said that the scene even managed to retrieve her lost sense of humour. 'The first thought that came to my mind was: If you're going to imitate Jesus, at least, do a more refined job of it. In that moment, as the fake fog cleared the room and the faux Jesus glided across the aisles, my mind cleared of its sickness and I was ready to run back home. I didn't want to stay there a minute longer. I was healed and felt fit and fine. This guru had done his job,' Sophia laughed.

But the problem was that the only way to get to the top of that hill was in the retreat organisers' vehicle, and the only way out was with them. Moreover, it would cost her a fortune to hire a private vehicle to drive all the way up there to rescue her. This, when she had already spent most of her savings on this retreat in an unguarded moment when she believed that her broken heart would be mended forever and would start pumping again like a brand-new enthusiastic machine.

Till she sat in that fog-filled hall, Sophia truly believed in this miracle. But the clearing fog was also a symbolic shattering of her illusions about quick-fix spiritual solutions.

For a week, Sophia was trapped in that make-believe world where people pretended that the real world doesn't exist. They workshopped on various topics like emotional release, chanting, abstinence, and imbibing the guru essence into every pore of their being. 'I was sick to my stomach. I even threw up a few times because they were forcing these ideas deep into my head and I was rejecting them outright,' said Sophia.

'But lesson well learned. This group didn't work for me. I didn't realise that they were a cult when I signed up. Once I returned home, surprisingly, I didn't feel the need for more heart healing. I think the shock delivered in those French hills rendered less severe the pain of heartbreak. Maybe, that's their modus operandi?' she laughed.

Sophia is a highly educated, balanced, and rational thinking woman. If some great advertising can hook her with the promise of well-being, every one of us is bound to be a target of tall promises in the spiritual world at some time or the other in our life. The point is not to never slip up. It is about how to realise when something is not working, and how to take action to redeem ourselves, as

Sophia did. She may not have been able to physically leave, but, mentally, she was out of there the moment she came to her senses on the very first day.

Red Flags

Here are some red flags to watch in your own behaviour that should give you reason to introspect and assess the health meter of your relationship with a guru or sect or both:

1. **The first red flag to watch out for is your emotional involvement with the guru and the teachings.** A simple self-test to gauge your emotional involvement would be to make a list of the words that you use to describe the teacher. Do these words elevate the guru beyond her human status? Are the words mostly in superlatives and positive exclamations? Secondly, bring more awareness to how you feel within your body while talking about the Guru. Does talking about her make you tear up? Do you experience a racing heartbeat or an explosion of affection from your heart centre? There is no right or wrong in having any of these emotional experiences. But it is in your own interest to be completely aware of them.
2. **The second red flag to keep an eye out for is if you begin to believe that your guru's teaching is the only way for other spiritual seekers, too, and that there is no other path . . . and everyone else is fake and only this guru is real.** This belief has red written all over it. This is a tough one and even seasoned seekers could fall for this. It happens because the messaging from spiritual organisations is often convoluted. They

may not directly imply their superiority over other spiritual paths but could be passing on that idea in their teachings in more hidden and nuanced ways. But there are also many sects that are more direct in their messaging about their supremacy over every other path. Keep an open mind to look for this sign. If someone says that she knows the truth and only she has the path and the answers, run as far away as you can from her. Then remind yourself that there are different groups with different philosophies, all of which work wonderfully well. Each ideology has its role to play in society.

3. **The third red flag is that you take the guru's word to be final, like a decree issued by the divine.** Engage with the guru's teachings. That's why you are there. But also expand your own awareness and make space in your mind for various viewpoints rather than holding a singular and linear philosophy. Feeding only one spiritual philosophy creates a silo that eventually nurtures extreme viewpoints, which could be detrimental to your spiritual journey. The other end of this red flag also doesn't mean that you become an outright rebel, questioning everything that the guru says, and being that one person in class who argues for the sake of argument—and to waste time till the bell rings for the next class. Take anything that the guru says into consideration and reserve your judgment and faith until such time that your personal experience supports the guru's idea with valid evidence.

4. **The fourth red flag is when your close relationships—family and friends—see a change in you, but not necessarily a positive one.** When family members tease you about how spiritual you have become, laugh along. But if they express worry and concern about your changed mindset, evaluate their concerns. Is the change in you positive? Is your spiritual practice inviting new, positive energy into your life through healthy habits and healthier relationships? Or is it taking you away from moderation into an extreme lifestyle that would become not just difficult to sustain but also topple the balance of your relationships? Listen to friends and heed their feedback before assessing for yourself if the effect of your newfound spiritual path is having a positive influence over you.
5. **The fifth red flag is when you are spending way more time and resources for the guru than you had originally planned.** Are you ending up signing up for more courses than you had bargained for? Is all your free time being eaten up by the practice and teachings? Is your bank balance in jeopardy because of this new pursuit? Only you can decide what the balance needs to be. But this is a red flag worth paying attention to.

Spot Fellow Seekers Dressed as the Guru

While in social settings, peers can boost motivation and energy with their presence. One can come across self-appointed class monitors or teachers who claim to know deeper secrets. And they could, too. In one meditation group that I was part of, one man would confidently pick people from the group and tell them that their Third Eye was open, or that they were sitting on a swirling bed of hot energy. This sort of unsolicited information adds no value to the participants, but it establishes the one man as a leader within the group—as someone who can see beyond what anyone else can in the group. Gradually, those in the group would gather around him to ask for more information, encouraging him to talk about his knowledge and spirituality. This is a case of a wannabe guru who creates a mini group within a group. Watch for such Me-Too Gurus and be aware of their value to your journey. Just as you assess the guru's value, keep an open mind to the value of peers, too.

The Butterfly Effect

My friend Jon travels the world in search of esoteric experiences. In his search of almost 20 years, he has travelled to the deep deserts of Mongolia, lived in the monasteries of Myanmar and Thailand, met the healers of Turkey, spent time at the energy hotspot of Egypt, been to the temples of South India, and met the Siberian shamans in Russia. He is still searching.

And as I write this, he has been living in a cave in Nepal close to the Himalayas. Jon has had the good fortune of accessing these energy hotspots and meeting people who have dedicated their lives to spiritual work.

And yet, Jon hasn't been able to stop his search. He is looking for something and is moving, physically and emotionally, in search of that something. To put it simply, Jon is struck by the butterfly effect, in which even though a potent spiritual process is staring you in the eye, there is resistance in accepting it and in dedicating time and effort to the practice. Instead, there is boundless curiosity and the desire to keep searching, to keep learning about various spiritual paths out there.

Jon is on the exploration phase, unable to commit to one path and do the hard work. Although he is physically moving and gets to travel the world and meet these knowledgeable men and women, he is metaphorically stuck, unable to move his spiritual practice along.

The butterfly effect is quite the other extreme of blind devotion to one guru. It is about not staying with one path or belief system long enough for it to have any effect on you. It is about flying like the butterfly from one flower to the next to the next and going on a never-ending tasting course, sampling the offerings but not settling for one dish.

More than One Guru

There are many seekers who join several spiritual groups and have many gurus in different places. When with one group, they are completely immersed in the teachings of that guru, and, similarly, with another group. These types of seekers get the benefit of various teachings and also have the maturity to manage often conflicting viewpoints. One guru may disagree with a concept that another guru bases his entire philosophy on.

These seekers, unlike the butterflies, immerse in the teachings, follow the practice, do the homework, and are loyal to their gurus when with them. It is not possible to be part of more than two or three sects with this mindset. But such seekers benefit from their nonjudgmental attitude to learning. They are only there to learn and immerse in the experience, so what if one guru says meditate like this and the other says meditate like that. These students also have the pragmatism to not discuss, debate, or worse, criticise one path over another. They honestly believe that there are many paths to the truth, and even if it takes one leg in one boat and the second in another, they will play the balancing act to get them to the shore. This is a difficult task but, in the end, a beneficial one for the seeker given that they are not hung up on this guru or that path.

How Do You Know if One Should Continue Working with a Teacher?

Here are some questions that one should ask every few months, or as needed, while working with a guru or a spiritual organisation. Step back and reflect on your relationship with the guru and her value-add to your spiritual journey. Then answer these questions:

- **Do I know more than I did before I became a student of the guru?**

  This is a function of being more open and aware of spiritual practices. It is not so much about the technical aspects, such as the Sanskrit names of the chakras or mudras, for example. It is about a macro-level understanding of how energy works, what it means to be on the spiritual path, and how it benefits the seeker. At the very least, the student should have answers to these questions. Of course, these are the concepts that grow with time. But the student should be better off in her understanding than when she initially started the course.

- **Does the knowledge empower me to make better choices than I made before?**

  This is a subjective question. What constitutes 'better' choices? One way to answer this question is to find out if the student is feeling confident and is able to use willpower to reach her goals. Has the general trajectory of her life improved, bringing her closer to her preferred way of living?

- **Am I growing to be a better human being?**

  This, again, is subjective but needs to be answered. Is the student more empathetic, kinder, and more compassionate than before? Does she have greater awareness about humanity at large? Does she pay attention to service than she did before?

- **Has the quality of my interactions improved over the course of my time with the guru?**

  How often is the student getting angry or losing patience? And when she does, how does she manage it? How does she express difficult emotions? In short, is there a notable change in behaviour in the seeker? What does this behaviour say about her growth as a human being?

- **Do I have a greater appetite for spiritual growth now than I had before meeting the guru?**

  Does the student want to know more? Is she more curious than before? Is she bubbling with more questions, enthusiastic to find answers?

- **Do I feel like I am making good progress on my spiritual path?**

  Does the path that the seeker has walked since meeting the guru surprise her at how much more aware and knowledgeable she has grown to be? Is having the guru as a guide improved the quality and speed of her spiritual work?

- **Do I feel overall stable and empowered?**

  This has to do with the state of human emotions. Is the student able to manage negative thoughts, anger, impulsive behaviour, and compulsive acts much better than she could before starting on the spiritual path with the guru?

  The honest answers to the above questions will reveal if one is benefiting from the teacher-student relationship. If the answer to even one of the above questions is no, then the guru-student relationship needs to be carefully considered before proceeding. Leaving is no big deal because you, then, have yet another opportunity to stir awake the guru within you. And that, anyway, is the point of it all.

Time to Leave

Some seekers may find the leaving process difficult. The pressure to stay could come from their own thinking in which they believe that there is something wrong with their comprehension of the guru's teachings. They could be thinking that if they persisted a little longer, they might see the value of this guru-student relationship that the others seem to get so easily.

In such cases, it becomes important to remember that any spiritual journey uses both intelligence and emotions. It is a holistic experience in which the intellect is only one part of the learning process. The guru's teachings should resonate with the seeker for her to be able to continue that relationship in all honesty. If the resonance is missing, it is perfectly fine to find another teacher whose teachings echo better with her unique needs.

The pressure to stay on with a guru or a group could come from the organisation itself, as it does on many occasions. The spiritual organisation may try to lock you in for a longer period of time with membership deals and discounts, hoping that the teachings will eventually grow on you and you will stick to the habit. This is dangerous because the longer you stay, the harder it becomes to leave. And this is what most organisations count on. The earlier you rip the Band-Aid off, the lesser the pain. There is only one question to ask: Do you resonate with the teacher and the teachings? If there is even the slightest hesitation to answer this question, it is best to move on to another teacher who better fits your requirement.

Seekers, sometimes, feel weak and lazy to find other teachers. So, they make excuses to stick to what they have found. My friend Rati ended up joining a cult that was cloaked in the promise of openness and freedom but was, in reality, a suppressive environment of narrow-mindedness. They charged a mini fortune and kept members busy enough so that they wouldn't get enough time to review their relationship with the leader and the group.

Rati's heart didn't resonate with the group's teachings but she continued to attend the weekly classes and did the homework. When I asked her why she continued going there, she said that they had the occasional art class on Saturdays, and that they took everyone out to a volunteering session once a week. These were the only activities that she truly enjoyed. Rati was seeking an outlet for creativity in a spiritual organisation, and she was staying on for the wrong reasons. When I told Rati that art and volunteering were activities that she could take up individually, too, she replied that she actually found it difficult to leave and preferred to put up with the discomfort than speak up.

Rati, eventually, did leave the cult but only to join another one a few months later, this time as an employee. The aura of a charming leader, a demigod, truly pulled at her, and she was taken in by that presence despite having the discerning intelligence to articulate the mechanics of how cults work. This was an energy tugging at her heartstrings. The hope and promise of a better life are what resonated for her. And she adamantly ignored her intellectual reasoning to follow her heart's desire.

The art of leaving—a guru, a group, or any kind of relationship—is in itself a spiritual exercise. It is one that we practise daily and fail at many times before we succeed. But one thing is certain: Once the relationship with one's own inner guru is established, one will stop forming unhealthy relationships with gurus on the outside.

That is the point of all spiritual work, after all.

6

Navigating the Vast Spirituality Seas

'We shall not cease from exploration
And the end of all our exploring
Will be to arrive where we started
And know the place for the first time.'
—T.S. Eliot

I HAD ATTENDED A BIRTHDAY PARTY A FEW YEARS AGO where I didn't know anyone else but the hostess, Maitree. Maitree had made initial contact with me for a tarot reading session a few months prior and had lovingly invited me to her party.

At the professionally organised bash, I was led by Maitree to a table of women who visibly didn't mingle with anyone else but were attempting to make acquaintance within the group. They, like me, didn't know anyone else but Maitree in the party. As introductions were made around the table, I realised that these women were all connected, in one way or another, to some aspect of healing work. One was a reiki master, one was an astrologer, one was a crystal healer, one was a pranic healer, and another had attended several of these workshops with Maitree.

In short, this table was Maitree's spirituality table, and sitting here were her go-to people when she felt low, uneasy, sad, or confused. She had different healers to consult for different types of problems. But in most cases, Maitree consulted all of them, one after the other, for the same problem.

Maitree was not interested in learning any of these modalities herself. What she was willing to do, however, was to use the services of these healers to feel better, even if momentarily. The initial discovery chat with Maitree in the first few minutes of a consultation always went like this: 'I'm not feeling good. And I need to feel good right now. So, please help me.' An hour-long reiki session later, she would leave in a calmer state of mind. And then the next time around, a consultation with her would be more or less similar. Sometimes, it would go like this: 'I feel I have gained weight around my hips. Please make it go away and make me feel better.' An hour of reiki healing later, she would feel calmer, possibly more accepting of her weight, and leave.

Any attempts to encourage Maitree to start her own personal practice with any modality of her choice fell on deaf ears. She just didn't want to. She would attend classes but with the motive of meeting people who knew the technique. Then she would go to them as a client rather than self-service her own mind and spirit. What happened eventually was that her army of healers prioritised her level of urgency less and less. She was at the bottom of the list for most healers because one can cry wolf only so many times.

This forced Maitree to shake out of her lethargy and start to do the work herself. She started with a ten-minute meditation whenever she felt the urge to calm her overactive mind. She would instantly feel better and continued with this practice, albeit with erratic timing. In just a few months, without it feeling like a burden or a disciplined practice, she had started to spend 20 minutes daily on some form of calming spiritual practice, whether it was meditation or journaling or chanting. She couldn't deny the benefit it had on her state of mind. So, she kept at it. Then, she reached out to her healer friends only when she needed help with the heavy lifting of difficult emotions. And her friends more than obliged, adding her high up on their client-priority list.

It is simply not practical to pass on one's share of spiritual work to someone else to carry. We all have to do our own work. It is our own soul's work, which is too important to entrust with anyone else. While we find helpers, teachers, co-walkers along the path, companions, guides, and cheerleaders, nobody else can lift the burden for us. We have to do it ourselves. Seeking different spiritual means and endlessly moving from one path to the next in the hope of finding something easier is also futile because while you could always find something easier to do, the demand will still be the consistency of daily practice that even the easiest of modalities will need for results.

Moreover, going in search of a practice for too long is about using the path of avoidance. It takes hard work to keep up with a practice and stay consistent. Many of us would rather snack on different philosophies and paths, lying to ourselves that we haven't yet hit upon the one that resonates with our heart's calling.

* * *

Gitali had faced several challenges in just three decades of her young life. She had witnessed the death of her parents in quick succession to illness and had been in a bitter, abusive marriage. She knew that she needed to heal and went in search of momentary, feel-good experiences to healing centres and healers. She was keen to learn, too, and often listened with interest to everything that a healer would tell her. She would pay close attention to their language and manner of speaking and picked up some techniques by attending short workshops.

Before long, Gitali positioned herself as a healer and started to use the bits and pieces of knowledge gained from workshops to start advising people on their spiritual path. With no sustained self-practice or immersive spiritual study to speak of, this fly-by-night venture did more harm than good, needless to say. Nevertheless, seekers looking for answers still went to Gitali, initially. But soon, they wanted to look elsewhere in search of more depth and experience to their answers.

Both Maitree and Gitali's stories show that nothing can substitute one's own personal work and practice. The practice can start after years of aimless searching for the perfect path, or it can start today by realising that one is already on her most perfect path. But the practice has to start someday.

The Satisfied Bystander

In most spirituality-led social groups, there are always members who participate in all the meetings and discussions but only as moderators, asking questions for others to answer and passing on the answers for everyone to have. They don't speak much of their own practice or their personal experience with a spiritual tool.

Such seekers revel in the joy of simply being in the company of those who meditate regularly. They like to keep *sattvic* company and, somehow, feel that it is half their job done. A social outing to a café to talk about meditation with like-minded spiritualists or a silent walk at dawn followed by a sumptuous breakfast at a favourite restaurant could seem like spiritual events but they are actually social events with spiritually inclined people.

Unless you have done the practice in your own time and in your own company, whether in a group meditation or solo, it doesn't really count as work. There are many seekers who like to talk about practising spirituality and write off the talk as the real work. It isn't. It is the discovery of the theoretical aspects of the practice. But it isn't the practice itself.

The Curious Cat

Many seekers go in search of new spiritual paths and healing modalities to satisfy their curiosity. They somehow feel more informed and in the know when they have read the definitions of each modality and are aware about the teachers who offer the best classes in town. This is an information power trip. Every social group has such an information leader, who is nimble and agile enough to find out the best in the business.

There are many workshops and classes offered these days that cater to this very curiosity in the seeker. If you made an online search vaguely mentioning a spiritual modality, it is enough for the search algorithms to work on overdrive and collect the most attractive courses offered on that subject globally.

For the information hoarder, unless she does her daily practice, all this extra information is nothing but excess luggage stored in memory—unless it is her job to be a spiritual classes' aggregator. For members of the group, processing this ready information on classes and courses could become a burden that they were not prepared for. The new members in the group, especially, could feel underprepared to be part of this journey. The only way to tackle this is to ignore the overload of information. You may already have chosen a path and started the required work on it regularly. The curiosity to try another path may be too tempting at this stage when the group members talk highly of its benefits. Take their feedback into consideration but carry on with your chosen path. You can visit another path later once you have settled into your current practice.

It could be tempting to take initiations into various paths because of the fear of missing out. But you are not missing anything. Be confident of your chosen path and stick to it. The beginning of any journey, spiritual or otherwise, is always exciting and full of possibilities. But ask yourself if it is practically possible to follow several paths simultaneously. Your patience and persistence should be used to continue one spiritual practice.

The Sprinter-Style Junkie

SriVidya was part of not one but every possible spiritual group in her city, Bangalore. A bright and highly intelligent young woman, she was consumed by the idea of self-healing and spiritual work to the extent that she didn't pay attention to her material duties like earning a livelihood, eating nutritious food, taking care of her physical health, and having a balanced social life.

At any time of the year, SriVidya was to be seen planning her next spiritual retreat or rushing to a class. SriVidya usually scrounged for work that paid just enough to pay her basic monthly bills and enrol her for the next class. She was also overdosing on the different spiritual modalities and had, at one point, reached fatigue to such an extent that she couldn't carry on anymore. She had gained a lot of unhealthy weight due to bodily neglect. Her response to concerned friends always was: 'But I need to heal. I don't have time for anything else.' SriVidya believed that her spiritual work was the most important work of her life, and she was on the fast track to nirvana.

Spiritual work isn't above or below any of the other aspects of our lives, be it money, friends, or hobbies. And there is no such thing as a fast track to nirvana. SriVidya was telling herself that she would get rid of this most important spiritual work first and then she can live a free life, easy and light. And that is when she can focus on her other responsibilities.

Spirituality is not a sprint that will be over as soon as you touch the finish line. Besides, there is no finish line. It is a process of making life better, each day, adding quality to the day and to life experiences. Putting life on hold to be a spiritual junkie in the hopes of picking up on the rest of one's life years later is a lot like a smoker saying that she will smoke 40 cigarettes today and none for the rest of the fortnight.

Spirituality is a lifestyle, one that we feed into every day. And it gives us joy and calm and peace every single day.

Besides, the idea of being spiritual is romantic to many. Some believe that we are doing a job that is superior to other jobs, or that we are better than others who do not take up spiritual work. Again, this is not true. Each of us has our own life track that we travel along. And each of us does what is best possible at our individual pace and time and capacity on this chosen track of life. Our work is neither superior nor inferior to someone else's work. It is simply our own work and nothing more or less. The only truth while pursuing spirituality is to understand that it is hard work. It is a lifetime commitment that we must be willing to make.

When to Review the Add-Ons to Your Practice

You have a regular spiritual practice going, whether it is meditation, chanting, healing or energy work of some kind. You seek to expand or add to your daily practice. One good way to do this would be to go deeper along the path that you are already on. But, perhaps, a technique or modality that is unrelated to what you are currently practising has been calling out to you for a long time and you would like to explore it.

Here are insights that could help you with decision-making in your flirtations with different modalities and pathways on spirituality. These questions will help review your practice, and let you know if you should continue or revise your daily practice:

- Have you been spending too much time on your practice but not really learning anything that adds value? Maybe, the title of the course hooked your interest at first but then you find a lot of hot air and nothing of value for your personal journey? Don't hesitate to leave. People tend to hang on for too long when things aren't working for reasons ranging from guilt and ego to the inability to let it go. Remind yourself that it was only an experiment, and try not to take the results personally.

  Yes, you could deal with disappointment as, perhaps, the teacher or the teaching did not live up to your high expectations. But there will be other teachings that resonate with just what your spirit needs at this time. So, keep moving forward without getting stuck.

- Are you enjoying the new course but unable to integrate the learning to your current practice? Design your own practice schedule by making time for the practices that bring you joy. Don't hesitate to switch things around because the more important fact here is that you are enjoying the new exercises from your recent class. Make room for it because it is essential to retain practices that one truly looks forward to. Spiritual work needn't be a dry exercise at all. It is not about being serious and looking like we are about to walk through doomsday, not knowing how we will come out on the other side. Not at all. Spirituality should be fun and enjoyable, too. There are so many aspects of bhakti yoga that include singing, dancing, and generally making merry to express love and contentment. If this resonates with you, and you look forward to it, do this first before you get into yoga or meditation. Include other practices, too, that leave you energised and happy.
- Is your new exploration giving you opportunities to immerse in the joy of discussion? Not all practices are about doing. Many paths are also about spiritual engagement and debate to push the boundaries of intellectual understanding. If this appeals to you, then be aware that you are pursuing a course purely for its ability to be an intellectual stimulant. This is, however, not for everyone. Understand your specific need and stick around for intellectual discussions as long as they are adding value to your practice rather than draining your energy.
- When pursuing a couple of different paths, it is possible that you are unable to remember the essence

of lessons. It could also be that there is confusion over the contradictory teachings and practices. When this begins to happen, it is better to make the decision to choose one path and stick to it for some more time before expanding your learning. This confusion could be as simple as the different ways in which the same yoga posture is taught in different styles. For an intermediate or advanced practitioner, this difference may not matter as she may be able to perform both styles of the posture with ease and agility. Also, she may have already designed her own personal style of doing her daily practice. For a beginner, this difference may be too daunting and require her to go back to the basics and practice one path for some more time. Instead of being overwhelmed and sucked into the theoretical aspects of each yoga posture, continue the practice as your first teacher taught you or as you feel most drawn towards, and stay with it without further confusion or contradiction.

- Another trend that comes up when expanding the scope of spiritual practice to include other ideas is the tendency to dump the previous learnings always in favour of the new flavour of the season. Then, when the third learning modality comes along, one dumps the second for another flavour. This need for constant change speaks to the seeker's desire for novelty and freshness in practice. It is a dangerous trend because the seeker, then, becomes a butterfly having sampled several modalities without really experiencing even one deeply enough to initiate meaningful results.

- When working with many modalities and teachers, it is also possible that changing teachers and spiritual advisors too often can lead to completely cutting off from them. The cutting off can happen because of your need to move to another teacher, or it could happen because of the teacher's inability to accept that you are seriously considering other spiritual philosophies. It need not necessarily result in the severing of ties with your first teachers but there are strong possibilities of that happening, especially if you shared a strong one-on-one bond. It is best to be mentally prepared for this rift. A truly healthy teacher-student relationship is one that nurtures the student and encourages her to explore other philosophies and modalities. But if your need to expand your learning to look at other offerings is ticking off your teacher in the wrong way, then do your best to explain your need for wider learning. In any case, the fear of the teacher's reaction should not prevent you from exploring other modalities. Staying in a practice for fear of the teacher—and, sometimes, even terming this as values of respect and loyalty—would be harmful to your spiritual journey in the long run.

The Guru Aura

It is often tempting for the beginner to over-idolise the teacher and give her the status of a demigod. Exposure to a teacher with deep knowledge and understanding of a subject, especially in the esoteric space, naturally attracts respect and admiration. And most teachers are deserving of this respect, too, often having dedicated their lives to spreading positive messages and promoting healing.

Remember that most teachers are also students first. With the exception of some greats, everyone is learning and growing, albeit at different levels. The reason they are teachers is because they have spent more time on that subject; in fact, they have practised it for a long time—long enough to teach techniques and tips to others who want to follow suit.

Beginners, at times, tend to be charmed too quickly and too deeply by teachers who have a pleasing energy and a personality to match. It becomes all the more important to keep the balance in any path because the guru could be so enchanting that it makes the student ignore any red flags about philosophy or practice and follow that guru blindly, hanging on to her every word and command.

This excessive charm of the guru can have a reverse effect on the seeker who could otherwise be shopping around for more spiritual paths to learn from. In this case, being a butterfly is somewhat of a more desirable outcome than obsessively sticking to one guru, and that too for the wrong reasons. If this happens, ask if you are able to let go and open your mind to another teaching. If the honest answer is yes, then you are okay. If it is no, then work on a smooth detachment strategy to free yourself from this excessive attachment to the guru.

Seekers Who Research to Create Their Own Brand

Among your peers, you could meet floaters who study many different paths and under many different gurus, owing no allegiance to anyone in particular. This, sometimes, is a carefully crafted strategy in which they pick up valuable lessons from different teachers with the aim of devising their own practice. This is especially true for practices like yoga where research is ongoing along with the practitioners' study and work with it to design their own effective results.

Even reiki healing, an originally Japanese technique, travelled the world and has taken on adapted versions with local flavours. There is Sri Chakra reiki, Karuna reiki, Kundalini reiki, Jikiden reiki, and so on.

It is natural to be influenced by these floating seekers who may have more information on the many different paths and modalities out there. But when you do encounter their breadth of wisdom, ask yourself if you are on a similar path as them. Most likely you are not. Their reasons for being there are completely different to your own. So, bear that in mind when you interact with such floater peers. Your meeting them shouldn't become a motivation for you to also constantly hop from one class to the next, or worse, question your progress on the path thus far.

Back to the Basics: A Reminder

1. **When expanding on your spiritual work, identify your core personal philosophy, which needs to stay anchored.** It could be a value like growth or a goal like honest introspection. It could be something that you have borrowed from your recent spiritual learning. Based on this core personal philosophy, which is unchanging no matter which spiritual path you choose, ask yourself: What is that one modality or philosophy that I will return to, no matter the changing circumstances around me throughout life? This is a good grounding exercise to ensure that you are able to cut through the clutter of excessive information and return to the basics. This will keep

you moving forward along your spiritual path. For me, this core philosophy is oneness, and the modality that helps me enable this philosophy is reiki, the central point from which all my other work expands and grows.

2. **Choose how you spend your time on new learning.** Pay closer attention to the amount of time that you allocate to your practice and new learning. Then align this time allocation with your ultimate goal. The daily practice is something that you cannot compromise with. It is your anchor, and it will continue no matter what else you do with your day. So, now with the leftover time that you can dedicate to spiritual practice, choose wisely on how you wish to spend it. In this, rely on intuition to find out what could add value to your path and what is but a fancy desire. It's fine to work with fancy desires, too, as long as they don't cut into your core practice time.
3. **Curiosity can be an uncontrollable beast and can make you do things that you originally didn't sign up for.** Remind yourself that not every recommendation is suited to you. At some point in your exploration and expansion of spiritual work, one needs to stop roving and stay focused on the practice.
4. **There is a lot being said here about curiosity and the desire to know more.** But it could also be that you have no interest to deviate from your current practice. You are perfectly fine not changing it and going on with it just the way it is now. This is fine, too. But at some point, your practice is bound to reach a plateau in which it may naturally need a booster shot. So, changing things up a little and adding something

new could keep you motivated and give you revised goals to work towards. For example, in your daily yoga practice, adding new asanas to your routine works muscle groups differently than your body is used to on a daily basis. Or trying an extended guided meditation, in your meditation practice, that relates to your current practice might infuse positive energy to your work. But sticking to a routine without change, if that's how you like it, works well, too.

5. **It is but natural that at many points during your explorations, you will come across opposing points of view by different spiritual teachers or philosophies.** Don't rush to take sides yet. Reserve your judgment on it, and let your own experience, over time, reveal the answers to you. Living with this ambiguity is difficult at times but is also a spiritual practice in itself where you are learning to detach from the outcome of a debate. The truth may be delayed, and accepting that it will take time for the answers to be revealed is a way of paying tribute to all of spirituality and its lessons in the mastery of calm.

7

The Material and the Spiritual

'The Mind is chained to the material existence.
The Heart goes beyond.'
—Anoir Ou-Chad

One of my favourite analogies to describe the material-spiritual life balance is the string of pearls. I read this somewhere many years ago and it truly resonated with me.

Imagine a string of pearls, wherein each pearl represents one part of our material world. One pearl is family, one is home, one is career, one is car, one is money, one is friends, and so on. The string that holds these pearls together in place is our spirituality. Without that grounding factor of spirituality, the pearls would be strewn all over the place. They wouldn't sit together in a cohesive and delicately beautiful whole.

Similarly, the string without the pearls would be just that, a string. It is the pearls that make it an object of beauty. To be truly in balance with our material life and spirituality is to be like the string of pearls where one cannot do without the other.

What Does Spiritual Living Mean?

When one talks about living a spiritual life, the images that instantly come to mind are of a monk in deep meditation in the hills, a prayer altar, the burning of incense, and sacrificing a life of pleasure and enjoyment. If one is attracted towards any of these, she should, by all means, experience ashram living, attempt austerity, and delve into deep devotion. But to think that this is the *only* way to experience being spiritual would be a faulty or limited understanding of spirituality.

One of the coolest examples of spiritual living that I look up to is of my friend Pritam. One New Year's Eve, we both sat on my living room carpet, a spread of short-eats around us and each holding a glass of red wine, talking about the year gone by and the one that was to arrive in a few hours.

In that relaxed and unwound state, we spoke of aspiration, life purpose, ambition, and how they would translate to the year's resolutions. Pritam took a sheet of paper and rapidly scribbled a list of his top priorities for the year. Then he made a pie chart of these categories of his life. These included growing his business, investing in deeper and meaningful relationships, making time for reading, spending on favourite hobbies, and carving out more space in his life for spiritual growth.

Pritam has practised meditation and been an energy healer for decades. He has a well-developed intuition and is an empathetic healer who, in his fifties, is well placed to take up spiritual work, teach, and heal. But he wishes to stay at the centre of his wheel of life to balance its many dimensions. His pie chart, representing the wheel of his life, made room for material, social, and spiritual worlds to coexist in harmony.

As a business leader, creative artist, and healer, Pritam leads a most lively and exciting life. He does not wear prayer beads or use spiritual jargon. Instead, he brings his personal brand of kindness and compassion to every interaction, whether it is with business associates, friends, or fellow healers. He speaks with the same unwavering kindness to a security guard as he does to a CEO at a conference.

His equanimity and composure are examples of spiritual living, no matter the external trappings. He is able to maintain this outpouring of kindness because his inner light is always on.

The Spiritual 'Versus' the Material

Spirituality is often understood in relation to the material world. The material world firmly roots us in money, food, clothes, and sense pleasures. It consists of physical objects. The spiritual world consists of the mind and spirit. It takes us towards intangible concepts of thought, beliefs, and values.

It is unfortunate and misleading that one is pitted against the other in broad, sweeping generalisations. If you are motivated by the material world, money, fancy clothes, a big house, fame, and social recognition, the common belief is that a spiritual understanding of life holds no interest to you. On the other hand, if you are a spiritual person, delving into the metaphysical and doing deep work with your inner light, the popular perception is that you are not motivated by physical attractions and pleasures.

This binary approach is problematic because the material and spiritual lives are not competing against the other for your attention. It is not a 'versus'. Instead, it is a question of how much you have indulged your inner light irrespective of your level of interest or success in the material world.

Both the material and spiritual worlds coexist in every one of us. It is the world that we feed more that grows more. And we need to consistently feed both over the long term for balanced and harmonious living. My friend

Pritam understood this early in life and made a consistent plan to integrate spirituality in his largely materially driven life. He runs a successful company and could double his efforts to expand and grow with the intent of increasing the company's worth. But he made a conscious decision to devote time to the other parts of his life, too. And this is what made a huge difference to his life balance.

Pritam, today, has healthy friendships, hobbies, time for reading and a meaningful spiritual life, and it is only because he made a habit of it. It would have been easy for a young Pritam to direct all his passion and the temptation for success towards increasing his business and material gains. That could have certainly attracted, perhaps, a couple of bigger branded cars, holiday homes in exotic destinations, a larger troop of servants, annual vacations to far-flung corners of the world, and a higher rating on the coveted list of business leaders to watch. Instead, Pritam slammed the brakes at one point in his younger days and made the decision to spend time reading about subjects that were not necessarily connected to his work. He was investing in friends and meaningful relationships and was working on his spiritual life, adding meaning and purpose to it little by little, every single day.

Pritam surely found it difficult to make these decisions and stick by them. Along with reading books on latest trends in management and technology and searching recipes for making mulled wine, he was reading the Bhagavad Gita as well. When his peers and competitors were reaching new milestones in business, Pritam was investing in the quality of his inner world, and no external parameter can rate that quality for an individual but him. The result is that Pritam, today, is calm, balanced, and clear thinking in every situation.

The material and spiritual go hand in hand. They tango together. The material is the yin to the spiritual yang. The spiritual is the soil to the material seed. If the material is the candle, then the flame is that light given by the spiritual. And so it goes.

The thing to remember for anyone venturing into the realm of spirituality is that it has its own place in the world as do all the other important aspects of our material life. The material and the spiritual are the yin and the yang to our heart's vibration tuned to the cosmos. To reject one in the hope that the other world will take care of us fully is to be incomplete, and to not embrace the full extent of all that life has to offer. To reject either the material or the spiritual is to sample only a few dishes from the elaborate buffet on life's menu. Only when the two worlds come together in harmony do we feel fully alive and present in the moment. And isn't to reach that status of harmony the ultimate purpose for us all?

Understanding Non-Duality

The separation of the body and the mind, stuff and non-stuff, matter and spirit feels like a natural categorisation that is easy to compartmentalise. Seventeenth-century philosopher Rene Descartes identified these domains as separate, and this came to be called the Cartesian Split.

All things physical and of the material world could be studied by science and backed by evidence. The material world revolves around the ego. It is about our social standing, self-image, wealth, possessions, titles, and all that we have earned, even reputation.

All things spiritual, and of the mind, came under the realm of religion and are hung on the hook of belief. We are spiritual because we believe in such a concept. We also identify with a consciousness beyond ourselves . . . beyond our limited understanding of life based on our body and material wealth. Think of this as identifying with the unlimited vast space that surrounds us. This is called the collective consciousness. In Vedanta, believers identify with this vast consciousness as *Brahman*.

When we identify our individual self with this collective consciousness, the body-mind split disappears. Also, it is the mind that makes the separation of body and mind, matter and spirit. Without the mind, we wouldn't know the body or any material life.

This oneness or the concept of non-duality is called Advaita Vedanta. Vedanta philosophy believes that we have forgotten the non-duality of our existence and attract suffering because we identify with the artificial separation that our mind has created with the material and spiritual divide. All of Vedanta philosophy, therefore, is about helping us remember that we are Brahman—*Aham Brahmasami* = I am Brahman. The process of remembering that we are Brahman happens through yoga, meditation, and service.

The Wheel of Life

Another way to understand the balance between the spiritual and material can be done by visualising a wheel with many spokes. My reiki teacher taught me this analogy by drawing a stick figure at the centre of a wheel. The many spokes represent the different areas of life—parents, siblings, money, hobbies, romance, marriage, health, enemies, employment, inheritance, social world, ambition, education, etc.

Now imagine that stick figure walking towards one area, say romance. The wheel tilts from the unequal weight distribution and could even cause the wheel to topple. The same happens anytime the stick figure moves away from the centre. The wheel gets wobbly and threatens the balance of life.

This is the same with how we prioritise the many parts of our life. Focusing on only one area to the detriment of others is bound to cause imbalance, which shows up in one way or another, sooner or later in the native's life. To remain balanced, it is essential that we each stay at the centre of our personal wheel of life and from there operate every area of life with the importance that it truly deserves.

How to Identify if You Are in Balance of the Two?

It doesn't matter if we believe that we are physical beings undergoing a spiritual experience, or that we are spiritual beings undergoing a physical experience. Both have to work in tandem for us to live in harmony. Any imbalance in the two causes stress. But how do we know if we are in balance?

The very first step is to be aware that balance of the two is essential for well-rounded living. Any lopsided view of the material-spiritual balance is bound to topple our wheel of life.

The next step is to understand that our individuality is limited to the body. When the body dies, any notion of the individuality that we carried also dies with it. What remains is the qualitative impact that we have made on the world around us by leaving it a better place. This can be bringing more smiles to people, making them happier, leaving them more knowledgeable, and facilitating a better lifestyle.

A simple test of introspection done at intermittent intervals throughout life will go a long way to keep our awareness of the material-spiritual balance. With every big milestone in the material world, whether a promotion at work or a job loss, a sudden gain or loss of wealth, for example, ask the questions, 'How does this impact my spiritual life? What is this trying to teach me spiritually?'

An honest answer to these questions will set things in perspective and bring us back to the centre of our wheel of life.

Commonly Held Disbeliefs about Spirituality

Those who are too deeply immersed in the material world tend to scoff at anything spiritual, calling it metaphysical woo-woo and what not. The lack of belief coupled with constant negative talk—depending on whom they are spending time with—builds a wall of resistance to spirituality. Besides the preconceived notions, there are some commonly held ideas about spirituality, too, that often prevent the curious from digging in. Here are a few:

1. **The spiritual world is too arcane, secretive, mysterious, and often jumbled up in jargon and complicated concepts.** The very word 'spiritual' could set off the idea that it is inaccessible and too kooky to even understand. It feels like too big a mountain to climb. So, we don't even want to attempt to start the climb.

   People immersed in the spiritual world tend to talk—often overzealously—about energy, intuition, meditation, grounding, cleansing, and other terms that make no sense to beginners. This can be scary and put off many of us who are trying to simplify our lives and not further complicate it.

For most of us, religion is often the first entry port into the spiritual world. In simple rituals like lighting a lamp and chanting a mantra, we are trained to seek peace and stillness. But an attempt at understanding the symbolism and significance of our religious actions can lead to more questions as we dig deeper into our connection with the universe.

Understanding spiritual living need not be so complicated at all. The idea of spiritual living is about a life led by calmness, compassion, kindness, and acceptance. Like Pritam did. He never wore prayer beads. He immersed in the goals of business success, and at the same time enjoyed a sumptuous meal and loved his cups of coffee as well. He indulged in the arts. He lived with a pulsating awareness of every moment that made him alive and fully present all the time.

2. **The concepts of spirituality are not supported by scientific evidence.** To quantify something and to define it in a neat and tidy structure is essential for most left-brain trained minds to accept something. How a person feels or what impact a practice has on the mind and body over the long run are to be supported by science, often western-approved studies for some people to believe in anything. Such sceptics would selectively weed out the practices and belief systems that don't fit in with their logical approval process. This overreliance on western science and medicine has taken a different turn in recent years as research is making huge strides in covering the areas

that were previously considered a no-go. The study of biomagnetic energy fields and the long-term benefits of yoga, for instance, are adequately supporting some spiritual practices and bringing them out into the mainstream in a big way. But there is still resistance in many quarters to accept spiritual practices as having any concrete effect on the human body and spirit.

3. **Spirituality entails giving up enjoyment of life.** To many, the idea of spirituality means to give up everyday pleasures and live an austere life of minimalism. Every spiritual leader, and her followers, dress in a simple manner. They eat light and avoid excess in any form—be it sensory stimulation through entertainment or consumption of food, clothes, and daily needs. To those of us who are driven primarily by earning a livelihood, this is not just scary but also impractical.

   We lead quick-paced lifestyles and for this accumulating stress, there is also a demand for equally quick stress relief, which often comes in the form of delicious food, mind-numbing entertainment, and impulse buying that soothes frayed nerves. Spiritual practices like meditation and mind control take consistent effort and practice. Most of us are not ready to commit, therefore, end up telling ourselves that spirituality is not for us. And because we don't follow these common spiritual practices, we believe that we cannot be spiritual.

Many of us also believe that we are incapable of ever leading a spiritual life because we still enjoy our butter chicken, vodka, expensive perfumes, fast cars, and glittering gold jewellery. We are not ready to give up any of this. So, we tell ourselves that spirituality is too difficult and too much of an opposite to enjoyment.

While any form of spirituality certainly does not encourage excess in any aspect of life, it also does not take away life's pleasures. Spirituality injects a dose of calm and serenity that prompts us to assess our life choices and bring about a greater balance in our actions and behaviours. In short, we don't stop enjoying life just because we aspire for a spiritual life; we just, perhaps, seek enjoyment in a different place.

4. **Spirituality is for people who have failed at making a successful material life.** This aspect of spirituality is feared the most. It's not an uncommon belief that spirituality is the last resort of the 'loser' who couldn't make it in the material world or in the world of emotions. So, she turns to spirituality.

   The common unstated rule of life, which we accept and abide by unquestioningly, is that attaining material success is 'normal' and seeking a life of spirituality is most probably because we are 'abnormal' or have failed in the area of creating a 'normal' life. This sort of inherent bias makes a strong case for continuing to stay in the world of money, sense pleasures, and social acceptance while seeing spirituality as a polar opposite rather than as something that can be integrated to enhance the quality of material life.

   This belief about spirituality being a good fit for 'failures' in the world of money and success also comes from seeing many people turn to spirituality only when they have lost something very precious to them—a huge business loss, loss of a loved one, health issues, betrayal, or an emotional churning that rose up and caught them unawares.

Many, thus, resist going anywhere close to a spiritual life because it would then mean that we accept our shortcomings or failures in the material world. Instead, if we continue to push for material success, the hope is that we can stay in the world of 'normal' and never have to deal with anything else that is outside our comfort zone.

How to Balance the Material and the Spiritual

Integrate, not categorise. The integration of the material and the spiritual is already happening but we need to expand our awareness of it by understanding that we can only experience the spiritual through the material. The senses are a great example of this. We smell the scent of the fumes from incense sticks. If it is a scent we like and relate to, we feel certain emotions like calm and relaxation. The scent could also be a trigger for memory. It may remind us of someone or some place that we had been and enjoyed.

Similarly, with the other senses like taste, sound, sight, and touch, emotions are triggered. We taste the sweet dish offered at the altar. We touch the bark of a tree and feel its texture. We watch the sunrise and process the emotions that it activates in us. We hear the prayer bells ringing and sense a shift in our body.

The act of the sense experience itself happens on the material plane with the body being the carrier of the experience. But the outcome lingers in the spirit world, leaving an intangible experience that we can only express again through the material world. In that sense, everything that we feel and do is integrated both in the material and spiritual worlds.

When it is a matter of having too much of one and not enough of the other, then it is important to set the scales right. For this to happen, we each need to find out what it is that feeds our spirit and makes us come alive. For my childhood friend, Latika, it was art. For someone else, it could be travel. And for another, it could be designing spaces. The possibilities are endless but each of us has to find the thing that stirs our soul and kills the accumulated fatigue of the day.

Raja Ramanna, a nuclear physicist, was known as the father of India's nuclear programme. A science researcher of global acclaim, he often balanced the excessive material energy (pun not intended) by spending several hours a week playing the piano. He even wrote a book about Indian music. The notes from the piano were the manure that fed his spirit, and from there he was able to power through his nuclear missions. He had found his balance.

There could also be an excess of spiritual work that needs balance through material pursuits. Jeffery Archer, the popular novelist from the UK, has a regimented writing routine. To Archer, writing is his spirit work, and he also often says that he has no clue where his stories come from but they pop into his mind somehow. His creative and spiritual beams of light are open and thriving. He gets the balance to his spiritual world of writing, he told me a few years ago when I met him on one of his visits to Bangalore, through his social outings like playing golf, going to the theatre, binge-watching interesting western TV shows, and socialising with friends when he isn't at his desk writing.

One always feeds off the other. Each one of us must find what that balancing pursuit is for us, whether in the spiritual or material world, and make it tilt the scales of our life to a manageable middle at all times.

Material and Spiritual Fulfilment

The purpose of balancing the material and the spiritual is to feel fulfilment. Every time we satisfy a desire or reach a goal, fulfilment is achieved. Material fulfilment can be had when we feed off external factors, be it objects or people. At different stages of our life, material fulfilment keeps evolving. As a child, it would be, perhaps, to get warm milk just as we were beginning to feel hungry. As a teenager, fulfilment could have been to get our hands on a video game that we had always wanted.

As a young adult, the preoccupations are with first love and a desired job. As we grow older, desire takes on the need for expansion. Everything that earlier fulfilled us is no longer enough anymore. So, it takes on the role of a bigger house, dining at fancier restaurants, longer vacations to more exotic destinations, deeper commitment in a relationship, more sex, a better-looking body, a bigger bank balance . . . the list of desires is unending.

With these material desires, the control does not often rest with the one who desires. We are always dependent on several external factors for our desire to be fulfilled and for the goal to be reached. This puts us in a state of constant anxiety because of the number of uncontrollable variables. The only way to manage material fulfilment is to balance it with spiritual fulfilment.

Spiritual fulfilment is an unending well of fulfilment that is already available within us. In order to feel fulfilled spiritually, we do not need any external factors to work for us. We don't need to have control over anything else but ourselves. It is the mind's ability to get to a state of peace and calm no matter what else is happening around us in the physical world.

This is not escapism, quite the contrary actually. Spiritual fulfilment, or the inner light that enables us to see clearly both within and outside, shows us the real nature of our desires. We might still want what we want. But we are in a better position to assess the possibility of fulfilment, and also are able to manage the emotions that surround this fulfilment or the lack thereof.

Our minds are naturally inclined towards material fulfilment because we have trained ourselves to find happiness there. But lasting happiness comes from within. And an entire industry of self-help and self-care is dedicated to finding this kind of happiness.

The happiness that comes from spiritual fulfilment is not derived from anything external and is readily available to us always. And in more spiritual traditions the way to reach it is through meditation, contemplation, and prayer. It is the never-ending grace that flows through us. And to tap into it, our inner light must be switched on.

When the inner light is on, we can see not only the beauty and extent of the spiritual fulfilment that is already present in us, but we also understand material fulfilment in all its dimensions in relation to what we already have. This, really, is the purpose of all spiritual work. The material world must support us in spiritual endeavours as the spiritual world must feed the material world with meaning and purpose.

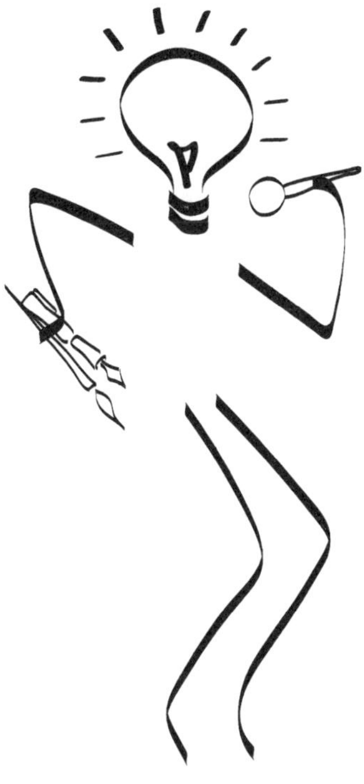

8

Creativity—
Where the Material and the Spiritual Meet

'The greatest spiritual challenge is an attachment to material things.
Even the most dedicated spiritual practice is meaningless when we are controlled by what we own.'
—Anthon St. Maarten

My KINDERGARTEN FRIEND, LATIKA, WAS KNOWN throughout school for painting the most soul-stirring images. She was bold with using colours but had the knack of bringing out the softest human emotions through her brushstrokes. Latika was always the chosen one who was sent to represent our school at various art competitions, and she often won big.

As a child, Latika had a quiet, observant quality to her personality that lent depth to her every move. She could meditate anywhere, and often had the smartest of solutions to our teen adventures. Cut to 20 years later, and Latika had made a big push towards material success. She had taken huge strides in higher education—earning a doctorate degree and now leading a prestigious institute on life-altering research.

In the years that she had spent focusing on building a career and gaining material success, Latika had not spent any time painting or meditating. Latika had an innate power to self-heal through painting. But in the peak years of her career, she had shut it down in favour of material goals like money, career aspirations, achievement, and success. There is nothing wrong with chasing success. But the balance on her wheel of life had tilted too much in favour of the material with no space at all for the spiritual, leading her to feel listless years later.

At one point, as she pushed 40, Latika had hit a burnout and was looking for answers. She wanted to know her life purpose and wanted to know why she was running around like a headless chicken. She knew that her body and mind needed healing but didn't know how to facilitate it.

I suggested healing through creativity. 'Why don't you start painting again?' I asked her. She hesitated and said that she hadn't done it in so long that she didn't know if she would be good at it anymore.

'Who cares about the art being good? You are painting because you love to paint, and it makes you feel creative. It is all that matters,' I told her, and encouraged her to take up painting more regularly.

We talked about our childhood days and how Latika had a special gift, which we now understand as magical intuition. Whether through painting, meditation, or her vivid dreams, this magical intuition flowed through Latika, which she could use to solve everyday problems. It also promoted lateral thinking. When she meditated or painted, she could reach a state of calm through which flowed both creativity and intuition. It was the same pipeline through which she could access a world of magic and paint those images. By shutting down this beam of creative and intuitive light, Latika had pushed herself into a corner.

Latika felt that she had lost access to that world and was not able to meditate or paint the same way again. After some encouragement, Latika hesitantly decided to make time and create art. The moment she held the paintbrush in her hand, her apprehensions were put to rest. Painting gradually took her mind off other stresses. She continued to paint not just when she had the time, but she began to consciously make time for it. Eventually, this opened up the beam of light in which not just creativity but also healing flowed with ease.

As it was with Latika, so it is with each of us. The manner of the creative spark could be different for each one of us. For some, it could be cooking; for some others, it could be music. But its purpose is the same—to turbocharge self-healing and creativity.

* * *

Each one of us is constantly healing all the time. We are healing from harsh words that someone hurled at us when we were vulnerable. We are healing from deep wounds inflicted by a betrayal. We are healing from abandonment. We are healing from physical, mental, and emotional infringements on our space.

But within us is also the power to self-heal. It is up to each one of us to get in touch with that part of our body and spirit that can activate the healing process. Often, when we go to a healer, this is what she does—get us in touch with our own ability to heal.

Creativity and healing are closely linked to spiritual life. But the beauty of it is that, like most things spiritual, it manifests through the material life. Latika used pen, paper, paints, an object, a subject, and her intelligence to create something beautiful. But in this process, it was her spirit that was fed and nourished. The beauty and inspiration from a rejuvenated spirit is just what Latika needed to pursue her material goals with a refreshed mindset.

The creative path could be material but the benefit is enjoyed by the spirit. In this, the two sides of material and spiritual are always interlinked, one feeding the other. And any form of creative self-expression is a way to boost the intermingling process of the material and the spiritual.

A Random Flash of Inspiration

When we think of creativity, most of us imagine it to be some mysterious flash of inspiration that hits us when least expected, such as when we are in the shower or when we are doing something else and not thinking about the problem at hand.

The credit for this notion of creativity, perhaps, goes to the story of Archimedes in the bathtub, hitting upon the idea of buoyancy and then running naked on the streets exclaiming 'Eureka!' The story is fascinating and makes for great telling, century after century, but it's highly likely that it wasn't even true. There is no evidence that this actually happened because the first known account of the naked Archimedes Eureka story was recorded by Roman writer Vitruvius in the first century, a good 200 years after it happened.

The inspired telling of this story, and other similar stories like the one of the apple dinging on Newton's head for the world to know gravity, however, made a case for romanticising creativity in a way that even today we see creative people as uniquely gifted and being at the right place at the right time, discounting much of the hard work, discipline, and rigor that go into turning creative ideas to something tangible.

Acclaimed American author Elizabeth Gilbert demystifies creativity, peeling its layers of enigma while rooting the creative process firmly in reality in her book *Big Magic*. She proves that creativity is daily acts of deliberate work and a lifetime of commitment fed by flashes of inspiration along the journey.

Spontaneous and Deliberate Creativity

There are different ways in which we can be creative. Neuroscientist Arne Dietrich researched these types and published his findings in 2004. Dietrich says that creativity can be different depending on where it originates in the brain. He created a quadrant of creativity and said that people can be spontaneous or deliberate in their creativity, and this can come from a place of cognition or emotions.

The four types of creativity would then be:

1. **Deliberate and cognitive:** The best example of this is Thomas Alva Edison's invention of electricity. There was no drama, no romanticised stories, only deliberate and consistent work based on knowledge to arrive at a creative solution to a specific problem. Cognition is important here because it shows that creativity cannot happen in a blank space with unknowns. Edison must know something about science to use that information to patch together the different pieces and arrive at a workable solution.

2. **Deliberate and emotional:** Finding a solution to a relationship problem can come from daily journaling, for instance. The daily act of journaling to place emotions on paper is deliberate. But when the aha moment, which strikes as a solution to the problem, comes from an emotional space—hurt, anger, or

sadness—it leads to a creative handling of the situation. You are allowing room to be deliberately emotional in a context. Emotions ride on deliberate acts to make creativity.

3. **Spontaneous and cognitive:** This type of creativity uses cognition, our knowledge of a subject. But creativity hits at the most unexpected moments. This is creativity that strikes when we are in the shower or driving or cooking, or doing something totally unconnected to the problem we want to solve. When the apple fell on Newton's head, Newton was relaxing under a tree, not thinking about gravity. But the spontaneous act of the apple falling on his head combined with his available cognition on the subject to give the world the laws of gravity.

4. **Spontaneous and emotional:** All kinds of artists, musicians, dancers, painters, and writers draw upon their emotions in the most unexpected and spontaneous ways to create works of art. Not just great works of art but also many scientific breakthroughs happen when spontaneity meets emotions, like a bolt out of the blue. Much of this cannot be explained. Who can explain the lilting voice of MS Subbalakshmi when she chants the *suprabhatam*, that quintessential morning song to wake up a beautiful dawn, to wake up the gods, to wake up our senses, to wake up when day meets night? Who can explain what emotions Vincent Van Gogh experienced when he painted the 'Starry Night' at an asylum in Saint-Remy? He was at a most vulnerable emotional state and painted 'Starry

Night' out of memory indoors when he would typically like to paint directly from nature when outdoors. One can only imagine the spontaneous and intensely emotional creativity that spilled on to the canvas in dark hues of blue contrasting with yellow to produce 'Starry Night'.

The Creative Link to Spirituality

Which of these above types of creativity link to spirituality? The short answer is: All of them! The more accurate answer is that it depends on how much one is indulging her inner light in creative work.

All creativity works at switching on and shining the inner light. But it is also true that the inner light brightens and enlivens creative work. Spirituality and creativity work together and in each other's favour, like perfect partners.

Every one of us is creative but at different stages of stagnant or active. When our inner light is ready to glow, often, our need to be creative is heightened. When our healing accelerates, we find ourselves gravitating towards creative work.

The reverse is also true. When we purposefully indulge in creative work, the inner light flickers and healing is triggered. When this inner light resonates with many more people, there is an inexplicable recognition of the emotions and the stories that are translated via creativity. This is the reason why one artist is liked much more by the masses than another even though both artists had similar training and environments to grow their creativity. It comes down to the way an artist's inner light glows to the outer world for others to vibe with.

Was the king of pop, Michael Jackson, spiritual, then? Absolutely, yes. We know that he was creative, producing music that resonated with millions around the world. But his musical talent overshadowed his spirituality. The late American basketball great Kobe Bryant famously stated in an interview published in *The New York Times* in 2014 that Michael Jackson got him to meditate. He said that Jackson could sit for up to seven hours meditating, and Bryant could barely sit for twenty minutes. Some of Jackson's songs reflect his sensitive and spiritual nature. They include 'Heal the World', 'Man in the Mirror', and 'We Are the World'.

All creativity and spirituality go hand in hand. It could be deliberate or spontaneous; cognitive or emotional, but they go together.

Allowing Creativity to Flow from the Inner Light

I noticed that my friend Keerthi, who was generally reticent and passive on social media, started to share images of her paintings. The initial set was amateurish but as the months progressed, she was getting better and better at the use of colour and the brushstrokes.

I congratulated Keerthi on her visibly progressing art work. We then got on a phone call and she told me her story. Keerthi had been trying to have a baby for over ten years and her attempts had failed. She had tried everything, including multiple rounds of IVF (in vitro fertilization) but nothing worked.

Agonised by this cruel hold of nature on her deepest desire, Keerthi developed aches and pains all over her body—a physical response to her emotional distress. 'One day, in complete surrender, I cried to Krishna to help me. I felt a wave of energy wash over me, something

I didn't recognise and still don't know how to explain. I suddenly took a pen and pencil and started to sketch. Then I bought paints that same evening and started to paint,' said Keerthi.

She explained that the moment she held the pencil in her hand, the designs would flow freely. 'It was as though I was led, by hand, by an unseen force.' Keerthi said that her body ache started to reduce with the painting. The more she painted, the less her stress and physical discomfort.

'Now, it is as though I am transferring all my internal stress on to the paper. I feel lighter, no doubt,' she said, and added that she still wants a baby. Her desire to be a mother hasn't gone away. She is still questioning her worth and femininity. But the art has given her an outlet to let off steam, and for that she is grateful.

When Keerthi discovered her ability to paint, a pathway appeared in which she could start healing her overheated system. Keerthi's inner light, which was overshadowed by her desire for a child began to flicker once she started to make art. The inner light showed her that she was capable of something other than motherhood, what she believed was her sole life purpose. The inner light lit up another parallel path for her to walk on.

Here, Keerthi first set foot on the path and then the light was shone on the path before her to see where she would be walking. Her creativity led her spirituality. And then she used her spirituality to infuse her creative art with meaning and depth. The inner light is central to this process, without which the two would be disconnected in their separate, disjointed worlds.

It takes courage to surrender to the inner light. At the moment when Keerthi said that she called upon Krishna, her choice of deity and higher power, is also the moment that she decided deep down that she was going to make a change in her thinking. Her conscious mind may not have processed this intuitive decision, but Keerthi was ready to make a change in body, mind, and spirit. That's when her inner light supported her and created a healing plan.

Singing off-Key but Hitting the Right Tune

In Keerthi's case, her spirituality triggered a spontaneous creativity. In Bhavya's case, it was the opposite. Her deliberate creativity awakened her spirituality.

Growing up in a strictly traditional Hindu household, Bhavya grew naturally inclined to Carnatic classical music. Her parents enrolled her in singing lessons from a tender age and had musical ambitions for her. The obedient daughter that she was, Bhavya did her best learning the ragas and the rhythm. But anyone who remotely understood music would be able to tell that Bhavya just couldn't bring in the emotion that elevated music to a divine level.

Bhavya was great with the theory but the notes would fall flat in practice. She knew this but the beauty of it was that she didn't care. She wasn't singing for social appreciation, accolades, or awards. She was singing to feel joyful deep within, to commune with her inner light, and her music achieved this.

It was her orthodox parents who forced her to sing in front of the guests at home and to participate in concerts. When young, Bhavya had an expectation that she would be appreciated but soon realised that she doesn't sing for others. She sings for herself, for her own joy.

She stopped attending concerts and foisting her off-tune music on unsuspecting listeners, much to the disappointment of her parents. But she was, at least, clear on why she was singing. Bhavya now sings in her own time, when she likes and how she likes. It gives her immense pleasure because the music has allowed her to engage with her inner light.

She first became aware of the inner light at a young age through music. And since then, she has realised that an easy way for her to engage her inner light of knowing and understanding her world is to continue singing. Bhavya's deliberate creativity is infusing her spirituality, a connection that a younger Bhavya wasn't aware of but an older and mature Bhavya, who is connected to her inner light, acknowledges and partners with.

Today, Bhavya sings for her own pleasure and to connect with her inner light. No other external force or person needs to engage with this exchange either as an audience or motivator. Bhavya, sometimes, goes into a trance while singing praises of Krishna. The important thing is that Bhavya is not trying to match any musical standard, nor is she trying to please anyone else. Her music is a matter of her engagement with her inner light. This musical feeding of her inner light has also made her more aware of her external world. Her relationships are better, and her self-confidence is in a healthy state.

For Bhavya, her music does not serve any purpose of profit, but it does much more to improve the quality of her internal life experience, her spirituality. Her deliberate creativity, through ragas, is adding ghee to the pot that holds her inner light. There can be nothing more lyrical than this for Bhavya.

How to Keep Your Creative Spirituality in Good Flow

Here are some notes to dip into your well of creativity to

ensure that your creative life is nourishing your personal spirituality:

1. **Your creativity is for your enjoyment. It is not for social media.** The minute you make any creativity with the aim of approval from others, you lose the joy of what it means to you, and it becomes a process of second-guessing what your online friends would like. Worse, your art will become a product to invite maximum thumbs up by strangers. But keeping this strict dividing line of art for self and art for others is difficult. The question to ask repeatedly is: Am I having a good time in the process of making or practising this art form? If the answer is yes, you are in a safe zone. If the answer is 'not quite', then you need to further let go the attachment to how the art will turn out.
2. **Find new ways to make the art fun for you.** Even art and creative work can hit a plateau when done the same way all the time, every time. I experienced this with drawing mandalas. After I had completed the pages of one drawing book full of mandalas, the process had begun to seem repetitive to me even though I was using different designs each time. I had to change up the process, use colours, use different kinds of pen, and experiment with different shapes to continue to keep it interesting. It's not difficult, but it needs a bit of attention and intention.
3. **Be unique. Don't copy another's style.** The joy of creating is lost when you try to imitate another artist unless the point is to create a perfect replica

of another art form, in which case the entire process becomes one of mastering a skill. True creativity is about creating your own art or music or free flow of ideas. There are musicians who are perfectly content with only playing covers. This is about your skill as a guitarist or a violinist. True creativity is about making your own music and enjoying the process of that creation.

4. **Meditate and then make art.** There is a vast space within the healing and arts that is loosely termed 'healing arts'. This category is at the intersection of the arts and spirituality, and it is aimed at enabling creative artists to get in touch with their spirituality and for the spiritually inclined to invoke their inner light through creativity. Often, these events are in the form of workshops, wherein the participants are made to meditate and then make art. Or they could be exhibitions of art, in which the artist claims spiritual inspiration for the paintings in the art series. To be absolutely correct, all art is inspired by spirituality. So, in that sense, all art is healing at some level. The healing arts category specifically claims that space and calls it out. I once attended a social meetup in which strangers to the city met with locals to exchange ideas and views. Among other interesting art forms on display at the event, a musician played a didgeridoo, an Australian aboriginal wind instrument made of hollow wood that produces soulful sounds conducive for deep meditation. The musician displayed his skill and created an ambience of relaxation, in which most of us closed our eyes and journeyed inward to our

inner light, whether we knew it or not. In that, the piece he played on the didgeridoo facilitated healing through creativity.

5. **It is not about being the best at it as long as it is fun.** When getting into a new learning, it can get tempting to invest in reaching higher and higher levels by taking advanced classes and passing exams. It, no doubt, gives a sense of accomplishment and also keeps you invested and motivated in the creative art. But if the entire practice becomes all about passing the advanced levels and less about the process of how you feel when you hold the paintbrush or pick up a musical instrument, then the purpose is lost along the way. Continue to engage in an art form because it helps you connect to your inner light and not so much because you get certificates and social accolades for it.

6. **Make time for the art, as you would for a friend.** When not motivated by a strict teacher or a specific outer goal, it can become difficult to keep up with the practice. One has to dig into a deep well of discipline and inspiration to keep the art form going. Even though you know that once you get into the practice, you will thoroughly enjoy it; life can get in the way if you allow it. Consistent and conscious practise with the intent of shutting out everything else to make time for your inner light, much like if you sat for a meditation session, is how you should be continuously engaging with your creativity. It is also *sadhana*, a deeply spiritual practice and a deeply personal one, too.

7. **Tap into your well of creativity to draw inspiration from it.** Everyone is creative, whether she accepts it or not. I once visited a friend in another city and wanted to attend this music concert but my friend was not very keen because, as she told me, she couldn't summon the attention and the intellectual calculation to enjoy the sophisticated piece of music. I was aghast at the very idea! To me, enjoying music was to surrender to its ebb and flow. But to my friend, an investment banker, enjoyment of music involved intellectualising the notes and the rhythm. I'm not saying that my way of enjoying music is better or that hers is not. They are just two different ways of enjoying music. The core of engaging with any creative art is to draw inspiration from it. I drew inspiration from music in a non-linear abstract, zigzag way. And my friend drew inspiration from it in an organised, left-brained, analytical way. Be aware of your personal style of engaging with creativity and see if there are ways to improve how it connects you to your personal inner light.

Think of creativity and spirituality as colourful rays of light flowing from the same source and connecting with the inner light in each of us. Our material world here is the cup that holds this light and allows it to overflow. To be spiritual also means to be close to our creative source and vice versa. It only needs awareness and the inner light to shine on this latent creativity in each of us.

9

Exploring Spirituality through Sexuality

'In the art of sacred sexuality, our bodies meet to physically express what is felt in our hearts and souls.'

—Michael Mirdad

No talk of creativity is complete without addressing our most natural inherent life force, our sexuality. The prude in us might like to cast it aside as though it is to be shoved into the darkness under the sheets, or worse still, labelled evil. But our spirituality and attitude to sexuality are interminably linked, and any beginner on the path would need to face these questions and, to make steady progress along the spiritual path, will need to understand her own attitude to sexuality. What complicates this discovery of our understanding of sex is often the mixed messages that come to us from spiritual leaders and guides.

Many years ago, my friend who was in his mid-thirties at the time was exploring Rajneesh Osho's teachings and had brought home a collection of books. His wife, more conservative with straight-laced thinking, was appalled at the sight of these books by Osho with whom she only associated free sex. The couple had roaring fights about his choice of spiritual learning. She thought that he was using these books to ostensibly explore trends in free sex, while he was genuinely keen on expanding his spiritual knowledge.

My friend tried his best to explain to his wife the need for spiritual exploration when he had the instinctive desire to walk that path. But the only thing his wife saw was that Osho's philosophy advocated free, wild, uninhibited sexual encounters with strangers. She imagined him having a string of affairs and their increasing domestic fights were based on her imagination of all that could go wrong if her husband read Osho's books.

My friend had to eventually give away the books to keep the peace at home, and shortly after this, they had their second son. So, sex was not taboo, clearly. It was only taboo to understand it, think about it, or explore its connection to spirituality outside the limits of sex's need for procreation.

There are numerous confusing and conflicting ideas about sexuality's connection to spirituality, and beginners on the spiritual path are bound to question the link.

In a Vedanta philosophy class several years ago, a fellow student asked the teacher, a senior ochre-robed Swamiji, for her opinion on the role of sex in spiritual exploration. Without batting an eyelid—but her cheeks going slightly reddish—she said, 'Avoid it at all costs.' She went on to explain that it does nothing but interfere with the spiritual process.

The student who asked the question nodded and then muttered, 'Rubbish!' under his breath. After class, the student told me he didn't agree with such a narrow view of sexuality, which is a crucial part of our physical make-up and such an integral part of life itself. 'We wouldn't be here if not for the physical act of making love! How can she say "avoid it"? Shouldn't we be working in active collaboration with our sexual urges?'

In another class, several years later, in another location and a different teacher, a student asked a similar question. This teacher, an 82-year-old sprightly man, answered with a deadpan expression, giving the question the same attention that he would to answering any other question. He said, 'Sex is extremely individual. It is a natural physical need. You are fine as long as you control it and not allow it to control you.' The teacher then explained that the sexual need is similar to our need for anything physical, including food and physical comfort like a good home, clothes, and secure shelter. 'If you forcibly deprive yourself, then how will you be able to focus on anything else? But at the same time, if you think only about sex and are obsessed with it, then you need to find ways to control the urge and direct it in more meaningful ways throughout the day.'

Walking the Line between Indulgence and Restraint

As this teacher explained, just as too much of anything is bad, the need for instant sexual gratification, too, can cross dangerous boundaries of healthy living and thinking. An increased spiritual awareness brings greater balance in every aspect of life, including one's sexual life. But a common misconception—most of it fed by what gurus say about the role of sex in spiritual living—is that sex is taboo and prevents spiritual growth or, worse, reverses it.

Many spiritual cultures avoid talking about sex and the few that do say that it needs to be removed from one's life if one needs to grow. The general perception is that all sex is bad.

But, more practically, many other spiritual cultures also recognise that sex is the essence of life. It is how we come into existence. So, to view it as bad gives us a limited or lopsided understanding of our world. Tantric practices, for example, teach that sexual energy is as divine as the energy of the rising sun, the flowing river, the swaying trees, and the rain-soaked earth. It is as natural as nature itself. So, to exclude it from our spiritual growth is akin to eliminating one limb from the growing up process. The result is a stunted body. Not integrating sexuality in our quest for spiritual learning will lead to a limited understanding of the path, forcing us to eventually include our sexuality in order to proceed beyond a point. But our own social conditioning could step in the way of an easy transition through the spiritual stages by taking along our sexual needs.

While you approach the role of sex in your spiritual path, be open to different points of view on the subject and reserve your judgement. You could agree with someone's view wholeheartedly, or you could arrive at an understanding that is a fusion of multiple points of view. The important thing is to ensure that your attitude to sex is not getting in the way of any other part of life, including spirituality. If anything, it should only boost your overall health and promote general wellness.

If there is any obsession, control, manipulation, greed, selfishness, and hurt, then the act of making love is not doing what it is intended to do. It becomes a tool of controlling another person to purely fulfil a physical need. If approached correctly, the act of lovemaking should make you feel understood, cared for, and appreciated.

When gurus talk of sex as a hindrance to reach our spiritual goals, it is often stated from a place of assumption that we are slaves to sexual pleasure and do not know how to manage our physical urges. Think about how this assumption works for you, individually, and then decide how you will create your own pathway to taking along your sexuality and spirituality together on your personal journey.

Creating a Healthy Sexuality-Spirituality Balance

We understand sex as a tool for pleasure and procreation but rarely as a path for spiritual development. This understanding of sex as a partner to spirituality is nuanced and takes time and patience to refine.

While in general, there is a clear separation between sex and spirituality as having two distinctly polar opposite goals—one is rooted in instant sense pleasures, and the other is about elevating to a higher spiritual plane—there are some cultures that have identified the connection between the two. Hindu and Buddhist tantric practices have traditionally integrated sexual energy into spiritual rituals and work with the two in tandem.

A lack of understanding of how tantra works, and the coming together of seemingly contradictory themes—sex and spirituality—have earned it a dubious reputation among the general public that haven't attempted to learn about it. 'Say tantra, and people think only two things: Black magic and sex. It's so wrong and gives the sacred practice a bad name,' a teacher of tantra once told me.

There are many fly-by-night teachers of tantra who use the sex factor to create courses and workshops that teach you to up your sexual game. An entire cult of tantric sex has emerged as a Pandora's box of secret tools to help increase physical pleasure. It taps into our curiosity and teases our temptation, but it's best to be wary of any quick-fix promises to transform your sex life.

I do know friends who tease those who attend tantric courses, attributing their relationship stability to bedroom secrets revealed in a tantra quick study. Again, humbug. The only way to ensure a healthy physical relationship is to base it on a strong foundation of emotional connection. Everything else is a stunt.

In my own learning of tantric spirituality, I am struck by the beauty of understanding the gods also as sexual beings. In our connection with these divine forces, tantra teaches us to integrate rather than ignore or separate these sexual energies. This perspective grounds our spirituality in reality rather than creating a divisive morality-led aspiration for seekers. It teaches us that we, too, are sexual beings and must accept what nature has given us and how we are made.

Here is how you can create a positive connection between your sexual life and spiritual growth:

1. **Start by laying the foundation for a balanced outlook to your sexual life.** Draw your wheel of life and rate the health of your sexual life. Just as an unhealthy family life or emotional balance would be affecting your overall level of happiness, an unhealthy sexuality would be interfering in every area of your life, not just spirituality. If you have rated your sexual life low, what can you do to improve it? Would it involve mending things with your partner or accepting your single status? On the other hand, when your personal spiritual outlook improves, every other part of your life, including sexuality, begins to look positive, too.

2. **Review some of your long-held attitudes to sexuality.** Do you believe that only the young, slim, and smart are sexually desirable? Where do these 'truths' come from? Investigate the root of these beliefs and negotiate with how they actually connect with the reality of the world. Other emotions like

shame and guilt could be piggybacking on these non-truths, further complicating your road to sexual liberation. Unpack them one at a time to uncover reality so that you can make a refreshing start with simpler truths and easy-to-manage emotions. This process takes complete honesty in self-reflection and the willingness to face some socially conditioned, unshakeable notions.

3. **Reclaim the innocent joy in sensory experiences.** Touching a flower, viewing a beautiful sunset from a mountaintop, relishing a glass of chilled pineapple juice, and indulging in fun finger painting can all be erotically arousing sensual experiences. Celebrate them all. The spiritually aware who hold a continuous attitude of devotion in their hearts connect these experiences to the divine. Sex should be no different. Just as these physical desires are spiritual, so is sex, as long as it is accompanied with the intention of sharing in a mutual connection. It is the beginning of experiencing the spiritual in all things sensual.

4. **Tantra believes that sexuality is a tool for your own evolution.** It already exists within you, and to deny it or reject it is to not use a powerful, erotic power that has already been handed to you by nature. Using your sexuality is about sensual pleasure as it is about flexing your spiritual muscle. The two are connected and cannot be separated. Erotic evolution is the path to our sexuality, creativity, and our highest spirituality. We only need to recognise how to balance it with every other part of life and not treat it as something separate or, worse, as taboo. Sexuality is already there

and has been given to us. To embrace it fully is itself being spiritual.

5. **Sex has been shunted into the performance model, in which the movements, act, and timing matter most.** This is done with the intent to derive the best experience, but if sex were to be understood as a pathway to spiritual ecstasy, as a part of celebrating our gifted life force and all things in nature, then our attitude towards sexual life would be different. We could ease into a meditative space and move away from the unnecessary social pressures for sexual performance that we burden ourselves with. Men, more so than women. Spiritual sexuality is about being conscious of the physical act as a pathway to experience a more encompassing peace and cohesion with the body, mind, and spirit.

Dissolving the separation between sexuality and spirituality is easier said than done. But the journey to understanding the split and working towards greater cohesion can be a fruitful spiritual exercise, one that brings us in greater balance on our wheel of life. When in doubt, it could help to take inspiration from our oldest human traditions, in which man lived in harmony with nature, remembering that we belong with the earth and are not separate from it. It could help to also remember that to acknowledge our deepest desires and working to bring them in greater balance is the best spiritual work we will ever do.

10

Religion and Spirituality

'To me, religion is an agreement between a group of people about what God is. Spirituality is a one-on-one relationship.'
—Steve Earle

Every year in August or September, depending on the lunar calendar, in the days leading up to the birthday of Ganesha, the Hindu god, I purchase good quality clay and head home to make an idol of Ganesha with my own hands. It is usually a slow process, considering that I work with clay only once a year.

But I usually keep the day free. I don't meet anyone on that day and spend time with the clay, first kneading it again and again while meditating on Ganesha, the portly deity, a personal favourite of many, including mine. I craft the idol slowly, first making the stomach and then the legs, arms, and trunk. I give him large ears and then spend time decorating him with flowers and an ornate crown. I make him sit on a lotus flower, which is also crafted in clay. I make little round clay balls to represent his favourite sweet dish, *modak*, and place it in his hand. Finally, and this is the best part of the process, I create a clay mouse, his personal vehicle, and place it near Ganesha's feet.

The entire process takes a few hours, the better part of an afternoon, because I am deliberately slow and attentive. This is my personal prayer to Ganesha a few days before He is welcomed in Hindu homes across the world.

On the morning of the festival, I install the idol at the altar and my parents perform the two-hour-long elaborate rituals, which are full of Sanskrit verses and incantations to Ganesha. At the start of these rituals is a process in which the spirit of Ganesha is invoked into the clay idol, after which it takes on the form of Ganesha himself, we believe. Then the flowers, fruits, and food are offered. We sing praises of Ganesha, do fire rituals, bathe him in milk and honey, and perform many ceremonies to appease him.

When this process is on, I usually sit at the back of the prayer room and watch in silence. I participate when asked to, for example, light the lamp, offer flowers, or say a prayer. But my connection with the idol was already formed and my prayer was already made on the day I crafted the clay idol.

To me, this is the difference between spirituality and religion. My personal experience of connecting with Ganesha was through making the idol. With every pinching and shaping of the clay, I was thinking of Ganesha, his form, his power, and his grace. It was between him and me. On the day of the festival, I participated in the rituals as a group activity through a community connection. My crafting the idol was spirituality, and participating in the festival of Ganesha was a religious experience. I enjoyed both thoroughly and in different ways.

Spiritual leader Deepak Chopra puts it well: 'Religion is belief in someone else's experience. Spirituality is having your own experience.' My connection with Ganesha while making the idol was my own experience while participating in the family festivities was the belief that this is how one is to connect with Ganesha. The celebration and rituals are based on a belief system that has been passed down through the generations, starting from a sage who divined the rituals in a meditation many centuries ago.

Both religion and spirituality have their significant roles to play in one's personal esoteric journey. The very idea to craft my own idol and to turn it into a spiritual experience came to me many years after I had been pursuing a spiritual path. But my initial connection with the Ganesha divine energy and my understanding of this elephant-headed God first came through religion in the form of these annual festivals in which I participated with enthusiasm year after year.

As a child, I was even allowed to have my own little Ganesha idol and perform my own prayers as my father chanted the Sanskrit verses. Being able to sit in front of an idol and do the entire two-hour prayer made me feel that I have a right to a special connection to the gods and don't need a via media. So, in every way, my link to the higher source was initiated by religion. But it was spirituality that personalised the experience for me, giving me the confidence to make it my own and go deeper in my journey. In that regard, both religion and spirituality have a unique place in my life.

Belief in a Higher Source

Taking the religious path to spirituality would mean that one is prepared, willing, and even wanting to be part of a community with shared beliefs and faith in the path. It is group work and faith in practices that the entire group participates in. With spirituality, even though an initiation may take place within a structured system, the work happens within the person, in isolation when the seeker goes inward and truly imbibes the teachings.

In that sense, religion reaches outward and spirituality turns inward. Whatever the path or form each one takes, both religion and spirituality believe in a higher source. The definition, understanding, name, form, and meaning of that higher source will be most likely different in religious and spiritual paths but they intersect in the primary belief that there is something bigger than us. It may be called Higher Source, God, Universal Consciousness, Divinity, or simply Inner Light. Believers of religion and spirituality agree that this higher source that is bigger than them exists.

From this common meeting point, the two pathways diverge into multiple arteries and a warren of lanes and by-lanes to reach that ultimate source. Although the paths may diverge, religion and spirituality are not exactly parallel tracks that never meet. They meet at the start of the journey, when a seeker chooses to follow religion or spirituality. The tracks also meet at the end in the belief of a higher source, an ultimate goal. There are many instances when the two meet along the way, too, converging at points of commonality. These could be with aspects of peace, love, equality, harmony, and other commonly held qualities across humanity. More than anything, the ultimate aim of both religion and spirituality is to eventually connect to the higher source.

The Choice between Collective Experience and Individual Path

Every beginner will have to take that first step into spirituality at some point. Religion is often a good soft launch into the world of spirituality, getting you acquainted with the practice of looking inward. One of the main experiential differences between religion and spirituality is that the former creates a collective experience while the latter focuses on the individual experience.

With following a religious path, there are structured beliefs and institutionalised rituals. There is a wealth of knowledge and experience from generations of following these practices. Every ritual and religious practice would have evolved through time to accommodate changing lifestyles but the core of the practice in most religions remains the same through history. This consistency and reliance on the familiar lend the practice credibility over time. The continued practise strengthens the religion through the years. Basically, it is about many people getting together to move in a common direction with a defined framework for being religious. Even if some of the practices and rituals are done solo, there is comfort in the community. Religious practitioners seek comfort in the knowledge that they are following a time-tested path that is approved by a large section of like-minded individuals.

On the other hand, spirituality is a deeply personal experience that focuses on the practitioner rather than on a guru, rules, rituals, or community. These outward motivations and triggers are less important when compared to what is happening to the practitioner within her own body and mind. Religion often promotes discipline, providing faith-based rules and conditions from which to operate. In doing this, religion triggers a deeply spiritual experience, making it a good runway from which to take off into spiritual living.

The External World and the Internal Experience

The spiritual journey is one that we indulge all on our own. For some, this solitary journey can seem lonely although it needn't be. For beginners, especially, the social experience of sharing spiritual notes brings solace in the knowledge that there are peers who think alike and are going through similar experiences. The sharing and exchange give comfort in the sense of belonging.

Religion highlights in its customs and rituals this very social and community feeling. It brings people together on the basis of common faith and makes them move towards a common goal. This group energy can be quite potent in motivating spiritual seekers to continue with their work and deepen their practice.

While religion projects the experience to the outside world through outfits, rituals, daily practices, and celebrations, spirituality turns that lens inward and makes the individual focus deeply on thoughts, emotions, and the profound connection she has with the power that is bigger than her. The journey inward may seem isolating and not easy to express or share. Religion steps in to fill this gap. But the purpose of both religion and spirituality, whether projecting outward or looking inward, is to turn on the inner light and engage with it at a deeply personal level.

Being Comfortable with Unstructured Pathways

One of the aspects of working with spirituality is that you will have to get comfortable with ambiguity, the unknown, and the unseen. Spirituality is never an organised, linear pathway that comes in stages, which are packaged in neat and tidy structures. No. Relying heavily on emotions, the mind and abstract concepts, spirituality is more often than not a vague world with as many ideas on how to navigate this world as there are people who pursue it.

Some techniques may work for some while the same techniques aren't as successful for others. This is where religion comes in to make sense of the abstract. The advantage of working on spiritual goals through religion is that most religions give tangible and easily relatable meanings to esoteric concepts.

In religions that believe in idol worship, the idol takes on the form of the inner god. The external idol sits as the manifestation of our internal divinity. There is a touch-feel form and structure to this idea. Similarly, there are rituals, customs, fasts, and observances to navigate the internal world through external objects and actions. Each religion has its own idea of how to navigate the internal world, and herein are the differences between religions.

The beginner on the spiritual path could find the concrete structure to an ambiguous pathway attractive at first. But the purpose of the rituals is to check in regularly with one's emotions and spiritual progress. Eventually, all seekers will have to deal with the ambiguity. Religion just arms us with tools like a torch and a road map as we go inward looking for our inner light.

You Have Got to Have Faith

The touchstone of religion is faith. Religion works only when its followers believe that its structure works, its stories are relevant to present day, and that religious practices are improving the quality of their life. Most world religions have stood the test of time and have offered solace and hope to followers by bringing meaning and purpose to life. Faith drives it.

Spirituality, on the other hand, is vulnerable to the individual's personal seasons of highs and lows. It relies heavily on the seeker's motivation to continue along the often ambiguous and arduous path. Faith to one ideal or idea is not expected of spiritual seekers because the individual experience is above the collective faith. What I feel and how I think are more important than what religion tells me to feel or think. This makes a primary difference between religion and spirituality. While the idea of freedom and the focus on individual experience sounds romantic, following a spiritual path brings its challenge of seekers having to endure periods of doubt and darkness as they trudge along the internal roads of their heart and spirit. Religion often has a faith-based solution to this kind of darkness and despair—say the lord's name. But spirituality seeks to find its own answers and work through the emotions to get to the inner light.

Spirituality via Religion

Here is what to expect when you choose to pursue spirituality through the lens of religion.

1. **Rituals:** Every major world religion has a strong foundation. In diving deep into faith, you might find meaning and purpose to religion like never before. You could find that reading the holy books and doing the daily prayer as prescribed by religion fulfils your every spiritual need. Stay with this belief but also continue to explore your inner world because while religion provides a pathway to spiritual fulfilment, rituals aren't by themselves the end result. *The outward projection of religious beliefs may be ignoring the inner workings of the mind and spirit. Become aware of this external-internal balance and try to bring*

it into harmony. The best way to find out is to answer this question: Are you spending all your time on the social and ritualistic aspects of religion and paying no attention to how you feel and whether you are growing to be a better human being? If yes, then your approach needs revision.

2. **Social aspect of religion:** Religion offers a complete structure that seems to be self-fulfilling at first. There are rituals, social gatherings, festivals, observances, and customs to follow. Religion draws up a detailed plan to keep us busy by giving us recipes to cook on certain days, the kind of clothes to wear, and the rituals to follow. These physical actions make us seem like we are doing a lot of spiritual work. But this is religious work, based on a set of ideas that is popular and has been given meaning through centuries and validated by the millions who have followed it. *Simply following this structure makes you religious but not necessarily spiritual.* You could get sucked into the big maze of beliefs and rituals of religion without really making the time to connect with your spirit and soul. In such cases, religion becomes a distraction to avoid going inward. Religion also gives one an identity that many people need, and seek, desperately. Seekers could be tempted to chase that ego-fulfilling identity rather than do the inner work. Know the difference.

3. **Fanaticism:** Religious believers who enter the fold at times of emotional distress tend to overemphasise the intangible benefits accrued through religion. This often tends to take such followers to extremes, making them converts in a fanatical way. The pursuit

of spirituality itself is aimed at removing imbalances and extremes of any kind to make us walk a harmonious inward path of awareness. In the case of fanaticism, religion comes in the way of spirituality rather than aiding it. This is not the shortcoming of religion itself but of the follower who elevates religion to that high status in her mind. At the other extreme, fanatical practice of spiritual acts also works against the seeker as it causes imbalance and tilts the focus towards one end. I once met a spiritual seeker at an ashram who would endlessly meditate for hours through the day, losing himself in the process, all because he was in a hurry to find peace. In this urgency, he was losing even the little peace he already had. *Fanaticism of either religion or spirituality is not favourable to leading a balanced spiritual life.*

4. **Too rational for religion:** Faith in another's story or a commonly held mythological idea may not go well with your rational sensibilities. If this is so, it becomes essential to separate the stories from the life lessons. But the stronghold of religion is in its stories. Faith in the stories is what makes the lessons carry far and wide. *If you are already prepared to do the inner work by wading in the ambiguous world, then you can bypass religion and head straight to your personal spirituality.*

Spiritual but Not Religious

This has become quite a fashionable term, a New Age anthem, for wannabe spirituals that use this term to dissociate from religion and any of its affiliations. Among those who identify as spiritual but not religious, which even has the acronym—SBNR—there may or may not be awareness about the fundamental differences between religion and spirituality. The primary motivation to use this term, in most cases, is to announce that religion is a bad word, and that they don't subscribe to its belief systems, structure, or practices.

In this rejection of religion, the SBNRs claim that while they don't want to have anything to do with religion, they are still spiritual people and believe in universal values such as peace and harmony. The interchangeability with which the terms religion and spirituality are used is the main reason that SBNRs specify which side of the scale they tilt towards.

What is so terribly wrong in associating with a religion? Every major religion has evolved with time to take on the new demands of a rapidly changing world. In being the touchstone of stability, religions have had to adapt in proactive ways to reach out to followers. These attempts by religion have spilled over into what's traditionally in the realm of marketing. More importantly, throughout history, religion has been used by political forces to further political affiliations and interests.

There are also fanatical streaks in every religion that paint an entire group in bad light.

These shifts in religion have tarnished its image or expanded its objectives, whichever way one perceives it. The SBNRs feel the need to proactively announce that they are not engaging with religion in their inward journey.

What does this mean for beginners on the spiritual path? The choice of engaging with religion on one's spiritual journey is a personal decision that is to be made weighing these different dimensions that every religion grapples with today. The advantage of using religion as a stepping stone to deeper spiritual work is that it is readily available; it gives form and structure for your practice; and it offers a social environment for beginners to feel safe and accommodated.

On the other hand, religion can also be too demanding on time and resources without getting to the core of the spiritual study in quick time. This defeats the very purpose of religious work. Every individual's case is different. But there are some questions you can ask to assess if religion is boosting your spiritual work or slowing it down.

- Are the rituals taking up too much of your time without leading you anywhere? Do you seek the meaning of these rituals but haven't found the answers, or the answers that you did find didn't satisfy your curiosity?
- Are social engagements central to your religious work? Do you meet family and friends during religious festivals and find no time for any personal spiritual work?
- Is religion demanding too much of your time and resources? Are you spending time and money that you don't have or could use elsewhere?
- Is the faith not agreeing with your rational mind? Is it too much of a struggle to stay in the fold when every pore of your being disagrees with what is being preached?
- Are the religious practices too complex to understand but you are being pulled into following it with the hope that one day it will all make sense? It could one day make sense, but if religion isn't easing your anxiety today then you need other tools, too.

- Is the practice of your chosen religious path excluding of multiple other paths, preventing you from even an initial exploration into a parallel path? There is, sometimes, a belief in a religion that other paths are not good, not relevant, or contrary to its own path. This could contribute to the seeker discarding religion in favour of a freer path.
- Does the priest as the middleman make you feel unfulfilled in your spiritual needs? The presence of a middleman, a priest, in most religions, can be a hindrance to one's own direct connection with the divine inner light.

The Link between Religion and Spirituality

As a child, I used to frequently visit a Ganesha temple near my childhood home. It was a large temple on a hillock that was several decades old. The temple was run by a priest family, in which every male member took on the role of caring for the temple and the several Hindu gods that it housed. One main priest was a middle-aged man who had shaved his head and grew a tiny ponytail at the back of his head as per the customs with priests belonging to the Brahmin caste.

This priest would perform the main temple rituals and oversee the working of the other smaller temples on this hillock. He had, perhaps, too many responsibilities on his fairly fragile shoulders, but every time I visited the temple, he was in a foul mood. His voice was gruff when he chanted the mantras. There was no gentleness, nor could I detect any devotion in it. If I closed my eyes and simply listened to his voice, I could imagine a man bitter with life and angry at the gods rather than praying with gratitude.

The priest's brows were constantly drawn together in a deep frown further adding to his aura of discontent. This man was surrounded by grace and divine energy all day in his work. And yet, there was barely anything to suggest that he was spiritual or connected in a graceful manner to the divine energy.

Another man that I came across many years later was the gardener in the apartment complex where I lived. He was also about the same age as the priest. The gardener, Sanjeev, worked with plants all day and hummed with a gentle smile as he worked. He truly believed in talking to the plants that he so lovingly tended to. He also had a ready smile for everyone who passed by. He spoke in soft tones, laughed a lot, and used humour to tackle any situation, whether it was a sudden worm attack on the plants or a cow that stomped on the new saplings.

Sanjeev was a staunch believer in God and religion, but he was not a ritualistic follower of faith. He told me one day that plants and nature are his religion, and God lived in them, so why look anywhere else?

The priest at the temple spent his days around an idol that was assumed to hold the manifestation of God but he himself was bitter, withdrawn, and unspiritual. Sanjeev, on the other hand, didn't care about setting foot in a temple but believed that God was wherever he believed Him to be.

The physical place and objects matter less than attitude and belief. Sanjeev's calm, content manner is not dependent on anything external. It is an inner joy that has sparked in him. It is his inner light that he has learned to switch on and work with. This light extends to the world around him. Sanjeev's spiritual journey isn't necessarily aided by religion. In plants and nature, he had found his spirituality.

* * *

Krishna Bhat's is a story of faith and spiritual living. The 86-year-old is a priest in the South Indian temple-town of Hampi. A 9-foot-tall Shiva linga, the phallic representation of Shiva, the Hindu god, stands in the course of a canal and is partially submerged in water. Bhat has been worshipping the idol every day for four decades by first cleaning the idol and then performing daily ritualistic prayers. Given the tall size of the idol and Bhat's own five-foot height, he steps on the idol and clings to it while cleaning it. Stepping on anything considered sacred would be sacrilegious but Bhat doesn't think so. He makes his own rules and says that his action is done with devotion, and intention is the only thing that matters.

Bhat's intentions are clear from his lifestyle. He lives a few kilometres away from the temple and often relies on helpful passers-by on a two-wheeler to drop him to the temple. He cleans the idol, performs prayers, and then returns home by foot. For this, he gets paid twice a year with rice and some money. But he is content as long as he gets to be near the Shiva idol. One doesn't know if Bhat chose this life or it chose him but he has been living this life for decades and has embraced it with devotion and joy. This is the highest form of spiritual living there is. He doesn't have qualms about bending religious rules because his heart's intentions matter more than what religion says. In this, Bhat has achieved the perfect balance of religion and spirituality. That's all there is to it.

11

The Role of Rituals in Spirituality

'Rituals are the formulas by which harmony is restored.'

—Terry Tempest Williams

When India went into a first-of-its-kind nationwide lockdown to slow the spread of the highly contagious coronavirus, I knew that the only thing that would make this uncertain time bearable was 'ritual'. I was going to miss stepping out every day and getting air and sunlight.

To compensate for all that I was going to miss, I devised my own rituals. My first ritual of the day as soon as I woke up was to open the window to let the summer morning air wash all over my skin. Then I would pinch a sliver of moist mud from a flower pot and smell the earthy fragrance, allowing it to seep into every pore of my body. In this ritual, I felt one with the earth, I *became* the earth!

Nothing else made me feel as connected to the earth as this healing ritual. It got my day going, and I felt grounded all day, no matter what craziness the day brought along. Similarly, I made little habits to follow through the day, and they became markers to check in with myself on how I was coping with the demanding isolation.

Rituals are designed to be physical manifestations of esoteric energy. Hindus circumambulate the shrine in a temple to symbolise circling around the whole world itself to show that the deity is their entire world. Then they turn clockwise in an axis to symbolise that God is within them, and that they are circling around that God within. This is a ritual that even kids observe and then imitate in temples.

It is, at first, a physical action to express devotion. But every layer of meaning is peeled away as we go deeper and deeper into our own inner light. We first question the action, then the mythological story, and then we test our own belief in it. With each level of questioning, we peel off another layer to explain why the physical act of circumambulating can mean the world to a believer and nothing more than a physical exercise to a non-believer. And that is the way in which religions turn seemingly meaningless acts into rituals—through belief, hope, a story, and devotion.

Rituals are so central to religion because believers count on the rituals' ability to shine our inner light bright and beautiful to light up the darkest caverns of our heart. Perform a ritual enough number of times and it will, one day, surely explode into a ball of light, removing ignorance and filling us with knowledge and wisdom.

Rituals ground us, their meaning and purpose emerging in trickles as we perform them with more awareness. Not all rituals are mythological or merely physical acts testing the seeker's intent. Many rituals were devised as shields for environmental factors, seasonal changes, and to strengthen our body and mind. While many rituals may have become irrelevant today, they continue to be carried in the believers' hearts as powerful manifestations that served an earlier time quite wonderfully. In their worse transformation with time, some are used as tools of propaganda and as manipulations to maintain a certain social order and hierarchy long after their usefulness is found to be redundant.

This is when rituals get murky and controversial. The testing parameter that I use often with a ritual is to ask if it can be personalised, and what it means to me no matter what the others say about it. I use it if it means something to me at an individual level, even if I only like the mythological story attached to it. I discard a ritual, guilt-free, if it seems pointless.

Myths as Carriers of Religious Power

I studied in a convent school and have grown up witnessing how religions can coexist with all their individual ritualistic practices. The school had a chapel, we celebrated Christmas with a host of events and plays, and the school held events to mark the various Hindu festivals, and days of national importance, too. The teachers were from different faiths, all meeting at the school with the common goal of creating an educated and aware next generation.

Etched in my memory, perhaps, because of her eccentricity, is my math teacher (let's call her Anuradha) who walked barefoot, had turmeric stains all over her body, especially, her cheeks. She pinned fragrant jasmine flowers in her hair every day and draped her saree at the waist so that it fell above her ankles, giving her the freedom to walk quickly without the saree pleats getting in the way.

Anuradha was a strict taskmaster and had a gruff manner about her that instilled fear and some amount of loathing in students. She wore her religious emotions on her sleeve along with a constant frown on her long face as she scurried about the school's corridors, barefoot and in quick leaps.

Steeped in Hindu religious work, Anuradha saw herself as a flagbearer for Hindu culture. She took her self-imposed duty of preserving ritualistic practices and beliefs rather seriously. This went to the extent that she looked down upon girls from Hindu families who did not believe in openly displaying religious symbols and affiliations.

A great proponent of culture and the arts, Anuradha taught classical music and dance, too. Her student once decided to perform to folk music rather than classical Bharatanatyam style dance at a school competition. Anuradha stopped the show, pulled up the student in front of the whole school, and asked her to explain her reasons for straying from the traditional, classical style. The student was in tears and was traumatised for her choice, which was only an innocent desire to try something creative.

I had my hair cropped in a boy cut throughout my school life and wore no symbols of faith, not even a bindi, that quintessential dot on the forehead to signify Hindu culture. Anuradha did nothing to hide her disapproval of my physical appearance, usually muttering a complaint as we crossed paths on the corridors and school halls.

Twenty years after I graduated from school, my classmates decided to return to school and thank every one of our teachers from kindergarten till high school for their teaching, service, and the indelible mark left on us students as we took wing around the world. The excitement of returning to school aside, it was an emotional day for many of us as we were also meeting our fellow classmates after two decades.

When I entered school that morning, so many memories flooded my mind in a hazy melody. I saw teachers and students huddled in different parts of the hall. I saw Anuradha sitting on a stone bench and speaking to a bunch of four, nervous-looking students. I was excited to see them but those hugs would have to wait till I greeted Anuradha. She looked at me with disgust, contorted her face in a deep frown, and pulled her arms up to the back of her head to gesture that I pull my hair up in a knot or tie it together securely in place. My hair was now long, and I had let it loose. I doubt she recognised me from my boy-cut years at school but all she cared about was that my hair was let loose, and Anuradha could not stand the sight of that.

'Some things never change,' my classmate whispered to me as I stood looking at Anuradha with no intention of doing anything to change my hairstyle. Sometimes, they get worse with time,' I whispered back.

Anuradha left quickly after we clicked the class photo and didn't join us for lunch that we had organised at a restaurant for all the teachers. She doesn't eat out anywhere. That was the last I saw of her. Now, frail and ageing, Anuradha hardly leaves home and has a troop of faithful former students taking care of her needs.

Long after the rush of nostalgia had settled, I wondered about Anuradha's persisting obsession with tied-up long hair in women. The belief is rooted in a mythological story, in several stories, actually. The one overarching theme is that of the tame-versus-wild dichotomy that women are slotted under, in an oversimplification of how women choose to style their hair.

Goddess Gauri, with a soft and benevolent nature, has well-oiled hair that is combed neatly and tied up. She even dresses her hair with flowers. Kali, the fierce warrior and destroyer of evil, has a wild nature. Kali's loose, unbound hair is a metaphor for this untamed ferociousness.

The epic Mahabharata has a story about Draupadi seeking revenge from Dushasana who dragged her by her hair from her bedroom before a court full of men when she was half-dressed and menstruating. Dushasana then attempted to disrobe her in full public view. Draupadi swore that she would tie up her hair only after she bathed it with Dushasana's blood.

In the epic Ramayana, there is a story about the kidnapped Sita sending a hairpin to Rama through Hanuman, the monkey God. The hairpin that held her hair in place was a message to Rama that her status and his reputation were at stake if he didn't immediately rescue her from Ravana's clutches.

All these references to hair may be in mythological stories but they carry the power of suggesting right and wrong, moral and immoral, good and bad. The imports of their meaning carry across generations over centuries, and even today we have believers like Anuradha tied to their faith judging women who choose to let their hair loose.

For many of us growing up in an even slightly religious household, these beliefs become emotional touchpoints. In most cases, we don't want to take a chance. *What if something bad happens if I disobey?* In other cases, it becomes a matter of keeping the peace at home and respecting family members who are staunch believers.

Often, there are no straight answers to why these beliefs stay alive over generations, but they carry the power to become matters of obsession. These beliefs become a bigger problem when they are imposed on others.

For beginners on the spiritual path, these questions can either trigger debate and engagement, or they can repel us away from venturing further along the path. But to make progress on the spiritual path, one has to deal with the ambiguity surrounding the answers to such matters that occupy the grey area of spirituality.

Ritualising a Natural Body Function

A big question that divides the believers and non-believers, and brings many of us in the middle of a slushy grey area, is why menstruating women are told to stay away from participating in religious rituals.

In my many years of spiritual exploration, I have come across people arguing for every side of the debate, even surprising me with their passion for it, especially from men who don't experience menstruation.

The first time I had my period was an unforgettable experience, as I imagine it would be for most women. My mother guided me on how to wear the sanitary pad and gave me minimum information on how often to change it. Almost all of it was left to experiencing it on my own and figuring it out as the months went by. Immediately after my first ever cycle at age 11, my mother called an aunt to visit, and the two of them made me sit in the prayer room and did a little ritual on me. It involved me wearing flowers in my hair and they holding a plate with lit camphor and circling it in front of me.

Apart from the initial limited information about how to manage my period, everything else surrounding the politics of the period was about upholding religious beliefs. I could not enter the prayer room or visit a temple during those five days. I was to stop all religious activity, and basically pause my life by doing the bare minimum necessary. I followed what was ritualistically expected of me. I wasn't going to rebel something that I did not fully understand.

As I grew more interested in spirituality, I naturally questioned the value in excluding menstruating women from religious spaces. My most progressive thinking teacher attributed this practice to a shift in energy. He said that women are more powerful when they are having their period. When that power mixes with the religious energy that we invoke, it can become quite potent and difficult to manage.

I heard similar explanations from energy healers from within and outside the Hindu context, even from foreigners who don't follow these rituals in their own culture. In recent years, at least, two teachers told me to follow my heart and do what I feel most comfortable with. They told me that there is no explanation to women's exclusion from rituals when they are menstruating, but the emotional weight of practising such exclusion all these years should not burden the seeker when praying. This made the most sense to me. And now, I follow my heart and my intuition on what feels right.

As should anyone who is confused about these practices and the rituals handed down to us in inheritance. Are they relevant? Do they serve our current reality? What does it do for me, personally? Ask these and more questions to decide how to proceed with diktats about rituals.

The Wide Grey Area

There are many similar issues that fall in the vast grey area about what is expected of spiritual/religious people. One contentious issue is the question of feasting and fasting. Fasting is integral to most religions, giving believers many options to be as involved as they would like to be. Hindus have the guidelines of religious fasting every fortnight on Ekadashi day, and then blocks of fasting on various religious observances like Navratri, Shravan month, and others. Islam advocates fasting during the month of Ramzan. Christians follow Lent to give up something that they like and thereby control the mind.

The culture of fasting is built into religion to offer opportunities for detox, better health management, and greater mind control. Fierce religious rebels tend to coat this intent with religious authoritarianism and domination. But the truth is that the followers may persist with the efforts and find their own individual niche of benefit. In other words, rituals trigger a deep internal change that gives way to a personalised individual relationship with one's inner light. This is facilitated by religion.

Meeting the inner light and engaging with it is delayed when believers get caught up in the rituals and elevate them to the status and end goal. Rituals are only a means to activate change. Getting entangled in them and refusing to see what they are actually showing us within is a reversal of the rituals' intent.

Many social rituals cross the lines of human decency and shouldn't be followed. Their intent was to create social divide and for the powerful to retain social and class power. But to paint all religious rituals as manipulative and regressive is to lose out on the many advantages of a religion-led introduction to your own inner light.

Questions about eating meat, consuming alcohol, and our manner of dress, for example, are all debatable. Beginners should be careful about whom to approach with these questions and how to process the answers. You will get a different answer from every single person that you ask. It is best to meditate on these questions, if they trouble you too much, and arrive at your own decision of what is the best way forward for you. And you don't need to explain your decision to anyone but your own inner light.

The thing about rituals is that they were created for a purpose at a time that is starkly different from the times that we live in today. We each have our own way to adapt the goodness of those rituals to our current environment. This should be a private matter, not one to be open for public discussion. The ones who discuss it publicly or try to explain what others should do are being political and not religious or ritualistic.

There is every chance that along your personal journey, there will be contradictions. It leads us to wonder what to do when our views clash with someone else's. A discussion or debate only matters when you seek more information from the other party, or if you want to change their mind about something. This process hardly does anything for your engagement with your own inner light. Sharing your experience with another is one thing but debating on which ritual or way forward is better is a whole other game altogether. Choose carefully, and decide if you would like to go down that road of making people think like you do and believe what you do. Ask why is that so important to you? All that matters at the end of the day is your own inner light, which you can kindle, grow, receive warmth from, and keep aglow. Everything else is a distraction, it is noise.

The Purpose of Rituals

Why were rituals created in the first place? They have had a strong place in society for as long as we go back to recorded history. Rituals have sustained in one or other form over time.

- Rituals give us something to do. They keep us busy. They keep us hopeful. Rituals fill our time with purpose and something to look forward to.
- Rituals float along an ambiguous line, in which we could only guess that there is some truth to their benefits, but we will never fully know until we tune in to our personal experience. Rituals are about producing a qualitative emotion that is at

the intersection of faith and emotional change. The benefits also depend on other factors like consistency in performing a long-term ritual and the expectation we have of the desired outcome. Even though it is difficult to establish a direct causal relationship between the ritual and a desired outcome, rituals could be serving other, unintended purposes like offering peace of mind, keeping us busy, and giving us time to introspect on the practicality of our goal-setting.

- Often, superstition and blind faith are mixed with ritual, causing many problems for rationalists who disbelieve everything that comes out of organised religion. In such cases, it is best to rely on your own experience and not go outside of yourself seeking answers. If you cannot find the answer yourself, trust that anyone else's answer will not quite serve your purpose either. Any sharing of experience about a ritual's benefits is extremely personal and is bound to be different for everyone. Understand this difference, create a healthy space by respecting these differences, and bring the focus back to your own internal life experience.
- Most of the positive outcomes of rituals rest in understanding how energy flows. This is a question of knowing the subtle body and being sensitive to changes within and outside. It takes most of us years of practice and learning to tune in to this subtle energy. In a bid to take a shortcut (there is no shortcut), seekers may look for answers from the more experienced in the field. But since this is an individual, experiential realm, the best that anyone can offer, even if a greatly respected guru, is sharing

her own experience. The rest is the individual journey that we each have to walk on our own.

What to Do When You Do Not Believe in the Rituals?

To each her own. Your own belief or disbelief in something is a private matter. Trouble starts when it comes out in the open and becomes available for social discussion. It gets even worse when your beliefs hinge on the outcome of these discussions and are open to change, accordingly. This means that you are relying more on others' opinion of a ritual rather than your own experience.

Whatever your belief or disbelief, it is best to keep things private. I read this quote about religion and find that it resonates with my understanding of the best approach to the vast world of esoteric knowledge. I paraphrase the quote here. 'Engaging with religion should be like wearing underwear. How comfortable it is, what it does for your important body parts, its touch and feel, and protection provided are all only your own business and nobody else's. Just as you wouldn't discuss the intricacies of your underwear with the world, you shouldn't be discussing your relationship with religion either.'

In the same way, I like to think of our engagement with our inner light as a deeply personal matter. We can share our experiences, no doubt. But to expect others to understand or to resonate with our journey is to set ourselves up for disappointment. Not only is it quite rare for us to meet someone whose journey matches our own, but also to continue in the same way with shared experiences is nothing short of a miracle.

If you don't believe in a guru but were forced to visit the ashram out of social obligation, then stay within the bounds of decency. It serves no purpose to diss their practices when physically present in an environment filled with believers. Remember the underwear analogy and strive to not show off your underwear to strangers or to those who don't matter.

I once faced severe judgment from a childhood friend, an extreme rationalist who thought that I was being naïve and wasting my intelligence on matters of the esoteric nature. His eyes were filled with a mixture of sympathy and disgust for my spiritual journey. He didn't even try to mask his views. But his thoughts and judgment were not going to add anything to my personal journey. I am on my individual path, and to expect him to understand it would be not only an unnecessary distraction from my path but also a useless debate that didn't serve anyone. I have a right to my beliefs and my friend has a right to his. To respect those rights is also about being spiritual.

This is something I wish my math teacher would someday understand. How any woman styles her hair is her own business and nobody else's. The world would be a much kinder place if we live and let live.

12

The Pilgrimage

'A journey becomes a pilgrimage as we discover, day by day, that the distance traveled is less important than the experience gained.'

—Ernest Kurtz

DRESSED IN BRIGHT OCHRE ROBES AND SPORTING A long silver beard, it was the turmeric paste on his forehead that dominated the old monk's face. He tied a bandana around his head, cut from the same cloth as his robes. He rested his right armpit on a Yoga Danda, a wooden staff, and held prayer beads in his hand. A copper water pot next to him completed the picture of a monk in meditation.

I wanted to click his photo but wanted to first seek his permission. As I hovered near him, he opened his eyes and looked straight at me and nodded, displaying proof of his prescience. I clicked his pictures from different angles, right, left, and even a dramatic low angle making full use of the soft evening light. He gladly posed for me, once in a deep meditative stance and then looking straight into the camera with starkly telling eyes. I thanked the monk and was about to leave when he held his hand out and said: 'Rs 50.'

I was had. We both smiled knowingly, acknowledging what just transpired. I pulled out my wallet and paid him but also stepped back at a distance to observe his modus operandi. The monk—now I can't say with certainty if he was only dressed as one but was really a monk—would observe the oncoming traffic of pedestrians and spot tourists with cameras. As they got closer to his makeshift seat by the side of the pathway, he would close his eyes and feign deep meditation. He would also know the right time to open his eyes and nod his permission to be photographed. When the job was done, he would ask for payback. Tourists obliged. I watched for 15 minutes how he baited to perfection every photographer in the market for an authentic click.

The annual camel fair in the western Indian desert-town of Pushkar is a photographer's delight. Every November, around the full moon in the Hindu calendar month of Karthik, the sleepy town comes alive in a burst of colour and culture. Camels, cattle, and horses pile into rundown tempos and travel great distances to be showcased to potential buyers. By the time the fair draws to a close, the beasts would have changed owners, changed village, or be cursed for not bringing in the expected money.

My visit to this event was going to be a spiritual, cultural, and religious affair. I may not have found many spiritual pearls of wisdom from the presumably fake monk, but he had other stories to share—of survival, practicality, and making hay while the sun shines.

As for my spirituality fix, I didn't have to wait too long. That same evening, the full moon shone on Lake Pushkar, when it is believed that all the gods descend on earth around this lake. Devotees make a wish for health, happiness, and anything that they need, and leave the lamps to float on the water.

The lake water was a bed of lamps carrying the prayers of the devout. And up above, a zillion stars twinkled like diamonds in the night sky. On the banks of the lake, make-believe priests peddled their expertise to tourists promising a positive energetic shift in their lives—a new life, a new destiny—if a certain prayer was offered on this auspicious night. I fell for one such promise, too, and sat by the water saying my own prayers quietly as the priest made a show of his elaborate rituals and loud chanting of mantras. I carried an inner quietude after this prayer and stayed with it.

Travel as a Spiritual Teacher

Travel can be a great accompaniment to a beginner's spiritual journey. It is not only fun but also a practical teacher, one that can set off an organic, real-life learning process. I believe that almost all travel is spiritual, whether it is an intentional pilgrimage or a trip taken for some time off from the demands of everyday life. Even business trips can be great teachers if only we open up to pause and observe the world around us.

In my many solo travels in different parts of the world, I have learned more about my own spiritual attitude by interacting with other spiritualists, at whatever stage in their journey they may be. Some of my travel has been intentionally for spiritual reasons—to give pause to my everyday drill and go within and reflect—while many others have been experiences that came along as I moved and travelled to see the world.

In that sense, the pilgrimage need not be a visit to a spiritual or religious centre. Every type of travel can be a pilgrimage to our inner light if we focus our attention there.

A hike in the woods can be spiritual if we carry that intent. This, I learned so beautifully by accompanying Evgeny, a 70-year-old Russian in Severobaikalsk, which is a town at the northern tip of the gorgeous and expansive Lake Baikal in Eastern Russia.

All along this incredibly raw and wild forest trail were scattered wooden sculptures of animals, including a cow, horse, wolf, pig, boar, reindeer, fox, rabbit, and a pterodactyl. Evgeny would stop by every animal sculpture and spend some time stroking its head or back, talking to it, whispering in its ear, and then plucking some grass off the ground and feeding it by sticking the blades of grass in its mouth. Evgeny was a man of few words but I saw the passion with which he spoke to the animals. There was reverence, love, and divinity in those moments, so I hung back to give him space for his very personal prayer.

With some animals, it seemed as though he was sharing a secret, and with some others he was persuading them to take care of their health. He used a gentle and calming tone when talking to the wooden animals in the fierce wilderness. There was beauty and balance in his actions and intentions. When I saw the wolf, a personal favourite, I fed her some grass, too, and whispered my message hoping that it would be carried through the winds and skies to the intended recipient.

This was such a personalised ritual that was impromptu, cared for the environment, and brought our awareness to our surroundings while connecting to the humanity deep within us. Even the biggest temples find it difficult, perhaps, to achieve this connection.

Evgeny showed me some of the local herbs, one of them called Brusnika (pronounced Bruce-nee-kaa), edible red berries that I had been adding to my tea during my time in Siberia. I craned my neck to look at tall pine, birch, and cedar trees; ran the tips of my fingers along broad, low-hanging leaves from young trees; and stopped to disentangle my scarf from thorny bushes on which were bursting fuchsia pink flowers.

When the thick green cover opened up to the landscape, I saw the railway track snaking through the forest and cutting through the urban settlement before disappearing into the horizon. At the top of the mountain, the silence was disturbed only by the low howling of winds. The sun shone bright, the breeze was biting cold, and sweat trickled down my back from the layers of warm clothing. Evgeny led the way down in his slow and sure-footed manner.

As we reached the end of the trail, my reflective sentiment stayed with me through a quiet evening and left a deep imprint in my mind.

Intentional Spirituality

As a visit to the woods can set off our spiritual side, so can a visit to a temple do what it is intended—envelop us in spirituality. Many seekers at different stages of the journey take arduous voyages with the faith that it will steer life in a new, more desirable direction.

My first visit to Thiruvannamalai about ten years ago was with this intent. This small temple town is famous for its hill, which believers give the status of the Hindu God Shiva. To walk around the hill, a 14-km stretch, is said to invoke the Shiva energy and our own inner light in a definitive way. So, on full moon nights, the most auspicious time for this circumambulation, devotees gather in large numbers and walk barefoot around the hill, propitiating the mystical and soaking in the inexplicable faith.

I wanted to experience this, too, and walked the 14-km stretch. My enthusiasm and curiosity took me through the first few km with relative ease. Then, as the time stretched before me, my legs felt like rocks and the end point—Arunachaleswarar temple—seemed further and further away. Every step became more arduous as the soles of my bare feet crunched the tiny gravel strewn on the road and the pavement. They pierced my feet like millions of pinpricks and sent shooting waves of pain up my legs. It was inevitable to ask myself why I was doing this. The fact is that I didn't know. I was led by faith, and it was best to not explain it. All I could do was carry on, and I did.

As I entered the temple three hours later at the end of the 14-km walk, I was in a vulnerable state of mind. It was one of total surrender, a state that I imagine would be difficult to achieve without that arduous walk. My mind was prepared for this walk, and the exertion on the body. But it was my faith that gave a boost to both the mind and body to carry on and complete the task. I felt a happy sense of achievement at the end of that journey and felt like a changed person, too, in a way that I cannot exactly pinpoint. Some things are best left unexplained.

How Beginners on the Spiritual Path Can Optimise Travel Experiences

Travel can be a valuable partner to our spiritual journey. Here are gems from my own travel experiences that allowed me to embrace a mindset that enriched my spiritual world:

1. **Be open. Expect the unexpected.** Travel often throws surprises our way. Embrace them and flow like water.
2. **Keep an open mind to synchronicity.** Look up and outside of your phone or book. Observe the world go by. Notice the plants and the colour of the sky. Watch people as they go about their daily lives.

3. **Laugh a lot.** Pilgrimages need not be grim affairs. On my walk in Thiruvannamalai, I saw large groups of devotees singing, dancing, and making merry while doing the walk. It need not be a walk of torture at all. It can be a walk of fun as the devotees showed so beautifully.
4. **Be present in the moment and engage all your senses in the experience.** Reflecting on life—looking back and looking ahead—are fine. But much of the joy of travel comes from leaving the past behind and being in the present moment. Travel's sensorial experience makes this easier. A different environment and a new experience can change how we understand the world.

The path to the inner light can also come from walking a less trodden path in the outer world. Travel can facilitate this beautifully. For beginners, this can be a great way to start a personal spiritual journey towards the inner light.

It sounds like an irony—to move outward while we actually want to activate the inner world. Travel is capable of being that link between the journey to physical destinations as well as the voyage deep into one's heart. Sometimes, lighting a fire in a dense forest at dusk can make our inner light flicker bright. That one moment can light up our life like nothing else can. Every pilgrimage is, in some ways, the search of one such life-changing moment.

13

The Social Spirituals

'It's easier to fool people than to convince them that they have been fooled.'

—Mark Twain

FORTY-TWO-YEAR-OLD REVATI ENROLLED FOR A reiki healing class four years ago as part of her effort to overcome a relationship break-up that devastated her stability. At class, she met Chitra, and the two became good friends. They would spend a lot of time together post class to discuss course work and life. Chitra had been shopping for spirituality classes longer than Revati had, and in the course of their conversations, she introduced Revati to several other modalities in the healing and spiritual space.

On Chitra's recommendation, Revati enrolled for a class on pranic healing, where she met Sadhana. The two got on like a house on fire. Sadhana introduced Revati to her group of friends, who met socially at cafes and in each other's homes for potlucks. They mostly discussed energy work and spirituality as they bit into pizza and sipped on organic tea. Revati started to gradually move away from Chitra and spent more time with this new group of spirituals, with whom she felt alive and happy. Listening to this group share stories of magical healing and the many miraculous wonders of spirituality felt like soothing balm to her aching heart. Revati found hope once again, and her emotions opened up to feeling more deeply once more.

Being in the midst of believers, healers, dreamers, and poets gave Revati fresh wind beneath her wings and new hope to her aspirations. She had opened up to a magical world that she, till now, believed only existed in storybooks. Her mind was absorbing a lot of information about so many modalities, whether it was reiki, pranic healing, crystal healing, shamanism, Bach flower remedies, energy medicine, yogic therapy, acupressure, or Akashic records. Revati felt privileged to be in the know and to be part of the inner circle of a group that had advanced knowledge of this magic.

A few weeks later, Revati signed up for a philosophy class where she met Praniti, who told her about shamanism. Gradually, Revati discovered more about Praniti's journey and the teachers that she recommended. She was now curious and dipped into learning about shamanism, too. Fascinated with all that she was learning, Revati had an explosion of sorts into the world of spirituality while continuing her exploration along several pathways at once.

Over four years, Revati collected many tools of spirituality and healing. Her meeting Chitra, Sadhana, and Praniti and through them the many others who were neck-deep in this world of magic, made Revati feel a special confidence that she thought she had lost to her supposed failures.

Revati now had information on her fingertips. She was aware of different practices and therapies and had attended, at least, one introductory workshop in each practice. She could speak confidently about the different modalities and how each was unique. Revati's appetite for spiritual work was fed by the people that she spent time with. She could meditate and do the practice when she attended class or met people in groups.

But when it was time to practice what she had learned in these various workshops, Revati found it difficult to hold her attention. She found it difficult to sit alone and by herself even for a short meditation. She needed to sit with people around her; she needed to hear the group chatter before they sat to meditate; and immediately after the work was done, she needed to plunge right back into group conversation. In her search for social company to do the work, Revati had, along the way, made many friends with similar spiritual interests. But in fulfilling this social parameter for spiritual work, she had neglected to practise sitting in comfort with herself.

For Revati, the presence of a group was more important than the quality or quantity of spiritual practice. A group session had become more important than the desire to go deeper at the individual level in any work. Revati was spending all her time gathering information and scraping the surface of each practice while marvelling at all it had to offer. She revelled in the joy of interacting with people, listening to their stories of healing, and learning about how different spiritual pathways can facilitate transformation.

But when it came to reaching her inner light, Revati preferred to seek solace in her social environment. This need for a social safety net is a trap that most beginners on the spiritual path could get caught in. It is a trap because while the social setting exposed Revati to the many different pathways and all that each one had to offer, she continued to stand at the crossroads without choosing to walk down any one path because she hesitated to walk alone. Simply gathering knowledge about the different options available to her seemed to be enough at that point. But it wasn't motivating her to do her own work. And without doing the work, there can be no benefit. What's the point of standing on the path if one is not willing to walk further on it? Along with gathering knowledge and information, Revati also had to gather the courage to walk deeper along one path, alone, and go beyond the social setting to turn inward.

The Importance of Social Groups in Spiritual Learning

Revati's desire to be a social spiritual is only natural. We are, after all, social beings. Revati cultivated her social network and now has the benefit of fellow seekers in the know who can advise her on courses and practices while answering any questions that she may come across.

In any learning, not just spiritual, there is power and potency to peer group interactions and activity. The social environment enhances the quality of learning and even brings fresh perspectives that, perhaps, even the teacher hadn't thought of. Healing happens through sharing and self-expression. When there is a narrator, there needs to also be a listener for the healing to pass between individuals.

All of the expressive arts and expression-based healing is based on this premise of a give and take. Healing also takes place in informal settings when stories are shared. Stories carry emotions, and when shared, they have the ability to be transmuted. In many cases, the mere narration dissolves the pain and trauma of the carrier who held those stories for years.

The social touch is powerful in spiritual and healing work. Even in one-to-one spiritual work, the presence of just that one other person can be a potent force in aiding the seeker to rise above negativity. The power of a social group in spiritual work cannot be understated. In meditation practice, it is believed that group energy doubles, triples and even quadruples, the potency of healing with the multiplier effect. This is the reason many spirituality cultures get together groups across the world to meditate at the same time to have a ripple effect of healing and peace around the world. They do work together at the same time, even if individually at their own homes, so that the energy of that work carries into the universe.

There are a multitude of benefits to social spiritual work. But to insist on it all the time is to miss out on the all-important inner work and healing. This is where Revati was struggling with her own work. She couldn't bear to sit alone and make a date with her own heart in isolation. While Revati got a great head start in spirituality, she stayed with the social aspect of the work without delving deep into practising the subject for individual gain. This, then, rendered the presence of the fellow seekers/helpers underutilised.

Group work is great for immersing in the collective energy. It does have positive effects that extend both internally and externally to the world outside. But individual work that one does in isolation—looking within one's own heart and switching on the inner light—cannot happen with the group. It has to be done by the individual through her own work and practise. The group may share words of encouragement and support while parting with experience notes, but the actual work has to be done by each of us in our own space and hearts.

Social Groups and Their Purpose

My exposure to social spiritual groups happened almost a decade after I had been walking on the spiritual path. Till then all my work happened only with my teacher. It was intense learning in which I was focused inward the entire time without any exposure to social groups. My experience with social spirituals was nil.

When I did make acquaintance with another seeker on one occasion, she introduced me to an informal spiritual group that had formed based on common interests and a friend who knew another friend. My first meeting with them was at a member's house for a group meditation. It was going to be a potluck dinner and socialising after the meditation. I was keen on the meditation and sharing the experience, but I soon realised that I was out of sync with the casual air in the room. The jokes and laughter travelled across rooms, and the members created a relaxed atmosphere. I didn't know what to expect, so I observed more than I spoke. Then, one man announced that it was time to meditate and we should all sit quiet. He lit a lamp and started to share instructions on how to meditate. I listened and did as instructed.

It was a short, ten-minute silent meditation. The man who instructed us at the beginning also gave the closing command. When we opened our eyes, he spoke about each one of us and what energy he could feel radiating from us at that point. Everyone nodded and went on to the next item on the agenda—dinner. This is when two outspoken women, out of the seven present in the room, started to share their experience with different teachers and healing practices. The rest of the evening that dragged on quite late into the night was a sharing of these different modalities and what each one felt and thought. While the two women spoke, the rest listened in amusement and wonder, asking questions and seeking more information. We ate in the midst of this conversation. I collected some valuable information on that evening, which encouraged me to try a couple of different spiritual practices with the aim of expanding my work.

This group met every fortnight for a few weeks before the cracks began to show. Within two months the group had disintegrated owing to power struggles, internal politics, romance, heartbreak, and jealousy. Everything happened so rapidly that, in just a matter of weeks, I was able to trace a few types of social spirituals that are most often to be found in any group. These types are to be found in every kind of group, with spiritual aspirations or otherwise.

As for my own engagement with groups, I had gone so far down the spiritual path alone that by the time I came in contact with groups, I was able to do my inner work irrespective of a group or any social environment. But this is not the case for most beginners, who invariably encounter group work in the early years. And when they do, these are the common types of social spirituals that they are likely to come across, especially in a loosely informal group created either by breaking away from a larger group or by bringing together seekers with common interests:

1. **The self-appointed guru:** This person is the group leader. She may or may not have the depth or the experience to lead the group but by way of years on a path or exposure to different paths, or even by the mere fact that she brought a bunch of people together, she takes on the role of leader to guide and direct the group. She takes the initiative to conduct activities and call for meetings. In many cases, she also claims to have all the answers to complex esoteric questions.
2. **The middlers**: These are yes-men who agree with everyone and everything all the time. They avoid conflict and don't question anything, even if it is

inconvenient to them. It is important that the seeker identifies them because they may not offer advice as per your best interests. Rather, the middlers will be keener to say the politically correct thing to keep all parties happy.

3. **The rebels**: As the name suggests, these members are intent on questioning everything not just to be the devil's advocate but to ignite the fire of differences within the group. They also rebel against the self-appointed guru and are often the reason the group eventually disintegrates. The beginner may find balance and a counter voice in the rebel when there is too much agreement and sameness within the group, indicating that it is moving towards a cult-like status.
4. **The opportunists**: These members are often the ones who step in and out as convenient to them. They collect information and leave. They don't participate beyond their means or interests, nor do they contribute much to the group by way of information or resources. In short, they are there to take and not to give. New entrants to the group should recognise them, too, for their astute deftness in slipping in and out of the group and yet maintaining their presence.
5. **The soloists**: These are members who often stumbled upon the group, curious to find out if working in a group is indeed superior to solo work. They are lone wolfs by nature and prefer to go their own way, often insulated from the happenings in the group. The soloists are among the first to eventually move away from the group, and are concerned only with their

> own path and work. They neither elevate anyone on a pedestal nor do they bring down anyone for their beliefs or actions. They dance to their own tune and log out of the group soon enough.

Many such loosely formed informal groups exist both online and offline. You would notice such trends in types of social spirituals even in large groups on social media. The choice of which type of group member you would be is yours and yours alone, but it is useful to be aware of these types of people, and to expand your awareness through observation. It, too, is spiritual work as it opens up your perspective and offers greater understanding about yourself.

Shared Beliefs and Philosophy

It is easy to form groups based on a common idea or belief. There are various spirituality-based groups that come together on the concept of, for instance

- **Rainbow children**—the belief that these children are born to guide humanity towards healing and to restore balance in the world
- **Starseeds**—supposedly highly evolved souls who carry dormant wisdom
- **Ascension symptoms**—the physical, mental, and emotional symptoms of a spiritual awakening and of ascending to a higher spiritual state
- **Bhagavad Gita study group**—the groups study and exchange views on the Hindu holy text
- **Meditation groups**—sharing wisdom and experience notes on meditation

The list is endless. There are also loosely formed groups that get together for satsangs and *bhajans*, where sharing is limited to the time when devotion is expressed through music and chanting. The groups tend to disperse quickly once the objective is fulfilled.

In all these groups, whether online or offline, the common idea initially brings believers together while the group takes on its own path of evolution over time. People join and leave and leaders may change. But for the most part, online groups have a large number of passive consumers who use the information and participate only when motivated to share an idea or opinion. Within such groups, the continued reiteration of an idea adds weight to the group's philosophy and keeps its followers banded together.

When a Group Attains Cult Status

The tendency of any spiritual organisation to turn into a cult must be observed by a beginner-seeker. The simplest way of identifying a cult is to check if there is too much of one thing in the group. Simply, anything in exaggeration, whether it is the demigod status of the founder-teacher or the group's foundational philosophy itself, is worth considering by taking a few steps back and reviewing the holistic view.

Here is a checklist of factors to notice in a group, which could be a cult or have cult-like behaviour:

- There is no room for a **contrarian point of view** within the group, even for a healthy discussion. Such views are instantly frowned upon and shut down like a tiny flame that could turn into a raging fire.

- **Recruitment** into the group is aggressive, focused, and business-oriented. If not monetary profit, there are other qualitative expansion goals for the group to recruit certain sections of society.
- Members of the group don't typically get along with those who hold contrarian points of view. So, they **socialise mostly with their own group members**.
- The leader has a **demigod aura** and is worshipped by the group members. The nature of worship could be different in groups. Some groups may openly use traditional symbols of worship. Others could use veiled methods like submission, giving the leader the last word on everything, and doing everything with the aim of impressing the leader.
- The followers are dead-sure of the philosophy that they endorse through the group or its leader. **Overconfidence** and complete faith in one idea is telling of the narrow-mindedness of some groups that refuse to entertain possibilities and probabilities.
- As easy as the entry into the group is, the exit is equally painful. The group goes out of the way to retain members through **emotional blackmail** and overextension of member benefits. This works much like a business scheme. If they are unsuccessful in retaining a member, they badmouth her and banish her from the circle for good, thereby setting a precedent for anyone else who could be considering quitting.
- Members believe in one idea, and that one idea alone. This is often by **criticising every other philosophy** or pathway. It is like putting one idea down to lift another idea up.

- Members of the group are often made to feel that they are **superior to others** because of their group membership. This is done by pumping their confidence levels through positive affirmations and building their image within the group.
- Membership to such groups often changes the world view of members, who begin to believe that they have found the secret to happy living, and that they are **smarter than everyone else**.
- This emotional play leads to a **loss of balance** in relationships, finances, and life in general.

Cults begin to operate as small, self-contained islands within the larger ocean of spirituality. Cults behave as though they don't need contact with the rest of the world. The members become carriers of this attitude—irreverence towards everything else but their guru or philosophy spilling over to everyone that they interact with.

Revati's search for the spiritual elixir first led her to navigate several spiritual paths. These were all centred on the social quotient of the group. Her spiritual exploration hovered with a cult, which gave her the gifts of confidence, emotional support, and the attitude that she is invincible.

Revati caught the signs of the cult but chose to overlook them. This could happen, too. The reason Revati preferred to continue her involvement with the cult was because the cult's work and its people were like a Band-Aid to her loneliness. She preferred to be part of the self-serving group because its members said nice things about her and gave her an important post within the organisation and made her feel wanted. This need to be liked and accepted is such a universal value that cults use these emotional needs as bait to draw in the most vulnerable among us.

Not just beginners in spirituality but those who have been seekers for years and even decades, too, could easily fall into the trap of ego-fulfilment. The important thing is to look for the signs that keep us stagnant and to shake ourselves up to keep moving forward. Any work on the spiritual path should keep our energy moving. The moment we feel stagnant, we can be sure that the energy is stuck and needs to be shaken up so it can move and allow new energy to flow in.

It doesn't matter whether this constant energy flow is facilitated by a guru, our individual practice, or a cult. The important thing is that we grow in healthy ways to expand our awareness about the world around us. It's important that we know what choices we have made by action or inaction. It's important that we know what we are responsible for creating or aiding.

The social spiritual group can be a wonderful partner in making us grow and thrive. But it's necessary to be also aware that there are manipulators out there who use our emotions to keep us stuck. At the end of the day, only we are responsible for ourselves and must take accountability for our actions.

As for Revati, at the time of writing this book, she was still with the cult.

Learning Is Great but Peers Are Average

What happens in situations when the organisation is great and the teacher is great, but one does not get on with the social group? This is a difficult situation to be in because the peer groups form an important part of the learning process.

In cases where all other factors work well except the people one learns with, it would be a waste of time to push through with the course. Unlike any other form of study, spirituality needs an environment that is conducive for learning, and this is not possible if there is toxicity in the peer group. If the group is filled with negativity, forming of cliques, and a general air of discord, then it is best to find ways to minimise contact with the group. Find ways to learn from the teacher in individual classes or with people who are friendlier learning partners.

The best conditions for spiritual learning are provided by the social environment. This might sound counter-intuitive to the idea that the most important spiritual work happens in isolation within one's own mind, body, and spirit. When the external to internal trigger for the spiritual work is led by a supportive and friendly group, the healing process is gentler and facilitates a lasting impact.

More advanced and evolved seekers will reach a stage when they are not bothered by their surroundings, and their singular focus is on the learning and their own growth in the process. Till such a stage is reached, every seeker must be conscious of surrounding herself with gentle and supportive partners in the spiritual journey.

Red Flags to Avoid Certain Groups

It is best to avoid a group or peers of your spiritual work when you notice the following warnings:

- You are made to feel excluded from the group based on differences like economic class, faith, or other reasons.

- Peers look down upon you for not knowing enough about the work, or for being a novice and asking too many questions.
- Or it could be the reverse discrimination where peers feel that you know too much and shouldn't be in the group.
- There is so much competition and one-upmanship in the group that it vitiates the learning atmosphere.
- You sense discrimination based on sexual orientation or personal life choices.
- You feel victimised indirectly through ostentatiously harmless teasing, which is actually indirect bullying.

Be conscious of these, and many other, types of discrimination that is possible in spiritual groups. They are, too, after all, made up of human beings with real emotions. There is a belief that spiritual groups are an oasis of peace and a zero-problem space. This is far from the truth. They are as vulnerable as any other type of group.

The pressure on spiritual groups to promote happiness and peace is huge because they are generally understood to be in the business of happiness and inner peace. But it would be wise to remind yourself that peace and inner work is your own responsibility, and any group or external teacher is only there temporarily to show you the way, after which you will be on your path. When understood through this macro perspective, social spirituals or teachers matter less. Yet, in the day-to-day, they are all important teachers and guides to show us the way to our inner light.

14

Spiritual Values and Activism

'Activism is my rent for living on the planet.'
—Alice Walker

ANITA WAS THE FIRST TO RESPOND TO MY REQUEST for a blood donor when my father was about to undergo surgery. I had posted my request on several online forums, including the business networking group in which Anita had seen the message. Not only had she volunteered within seconds but had also forwarded my request to other groups that she was certain would help. And they did.

By profession, the 30-something Anita was a government employee and spent most of her day in a bureaucratic set-up, moving files and preparing reports. But that was not how most people who came across Anita remembered her. Anita's ability for compassion, care, and empathy far outweighed any other aspect of her personality. Post a request to adopt stray dogs, and Anita was the first to facilitate a new home for the pets. Is there a friend in urgent need of a rental? Anita will activate her network in the neighbourhood and arrange something. A visiting tourist's visa needs extension? Anita will find a contact through a friend to find solutions for this stranger.

Anita would travel to remote corners of the country to volunteer her vacation time. She was no social worker but was one in every sense of the term. Anita may or may not realise it but she possessed all the qualities of a spiritual activist—taking the spiritual values of compassion, kindness, empathy, and unconditional love and turning them into productive actions to improve the lives of others.

Isn't all activism then spiritual in nature? Spiritual activism sets itself apart from other forms of activism in the process through which the end goal is reached. While compassion and empathy are driving factors to start the process of activism, spiritual activism tries to ensure that these values are sustained throughout the process and not just as a motivating factor.

What makes Anita's work spiritual activism is the manner in which she goes about her end goal. Anita speaks with compassion and kindness with every single person that she comes across—even if there is a perceived perpetrator or 'villain'. She may not hold placards and shout slogans to badmouth the big evil-doers, but she will quietly find solutions to improve the lives of victims. Even if her work is helping one person, she is content.

In spiritual activism, the work takes on an action-oriented tilt towards tangible results. It could be quiet, asking the question: What can I do to improve this situation? And the spiritual activist does it by standing true to the spiritual values that she abides by. It is application of the insights one gains through spiritual processes and reflection. In a way, it is an active, physical manifestation of the journey towards switching on the inner light or making it burn brighter.

While Anita is a spiritual activist for people, Jack is an environment activist with strong spiritual motivations. Jack lives in Canada and runs a spiritual centre that is rooted deeply in caring for nature and being its friend and companion. On his farm in the countryside, away from the hustle and bustle of city life, Jack lets nature grow wild and unmanicured on the land surrounding his wooden house, which is constructed using locally sourced materials.

Jack is a beekeeper and uses honey farming as one of the other ways in which to give back to nature by preserving and protecting it. Jack not only teaches his students to love nature but is a role model of ideal behaviour in sustainable living and giving.

The process of Jack's activism, quite like Anita's, is what sets it apart from environmental activism by giving it strong overtones of spiritualism. Jack doesn't insist on his students following his lead. Nor does he talk down to the people who come across as greedy or insensitive with nature. He doesn't let much else perturb his peace of mind. Instead, he says: This is what I do to retain my connection with nature. It is important because we have one earth to live on and must do what we can to preserve it. Jack doesn't play the 'You' versus 'Me' game by saying: You are doing wrong. I am doing right.

He self-identifies as a nature warrior but doesn't insist that others should be one, too. When asked, he shares his story. But not by talking ill of those who don't care for the environment. Even in the process, there is gentleness, kindness, and compassion. These are the qualities that set apart activism from spiritual activism. It believes that the process is as important as arriving at the goal.

Activism as an Entry Point to Spirituality

All forms of spirituality are about energy that flows. It is about learning how to direct energy to increase calm in the body and mind. This can be done by sitting still and allowing the calm to descend into the body and mind. Or it can be practised by increasing calm and gentleness through action. In the yogic tradition, this is called karma yoga, which is the discipline of selfless action as a way to perfection.

Activism is born out of this action-based spirituality. For beginners in spirituality, this is an option worth considering as a soft launch, an easy entry, into the world of compassion and empathy.

Spiritual activism gives you the flexibility to choose a cause that is close to your heart, or one that you feel strongly about. Then you can give of your time through body, mind, and spirit. Activism or any form of volunteering work is a leveller, working directly on the ego by expanding our awareness and bringing into context our place in the larger world that we inhabit. This is often an eye-opener and enough for most of us to start on the journey of self-discovery by delving deeper through meditation, self-inquiry, and contemplation.

While religion could help as an entry point to the spiritual journey, activism could help in it gaining momentum in the moving forward. In any form of activism, energy flows through the work and is exchanged with the people that we interact with. With every act, the ego is surrendered because the work is selfless. For spiritual seekers at any level, volunteer work can be a great leveller of emotions.

If unable to decide on a spiritual path to follow, it is best to choose a cause and devote time and energy towards that cause. From here, one can segue into spirituality by reflecting deeply on the teachings derived from the activism. Here are some questions to ask after a few months of activism work:

- What has the work taught me about the cause?
- Do I feel differently about myself? How so?
- Do I feel that I am more important because I do social work? Why so?

- How has the volunteer work changed my outlook towards life?
- Do I feel ready to learn more about myself?
- What are the biggest takeaways from my volunteer work on the following—
    - Time
    - Money
    - Relationships
    - Life purpose
    - Spirituality

Spiritual activism can play an important role in giving direction to restless energy. It can also guide calming energy towards immediate tangible results.

Being a Warrior

Most spiritual organisations have a strong element of charity or volunteering work. It is based on the premise that we are each an integral part of the earth and the cosmos. Not only do we belong to the earth but also have a connection with every other living thing here.

Spiritual activism works on the basis that every action and thought bubbles up into a collective consciousness that ebbs and flows with time and circumstances. Therefore, at the individual level, what we each think and do contributes to the nature of the collective energy that holds us together. Good thoughts and good deeds create a positive and strong collective energy, while negative thoughts and harmful deeds poke holes in this collective and make us weak.

As the world continues to grapple with Covid-19, different types of warriors emerged. In her own way, each warrior was a type of spiritual activist. Healers and spiritual leaders called for earth healing and set up common timings around the world when chanting and healing meditations would take place. People could join from where they were and participate in the spiritual activity with the aim of raising the vibration of the collective consciousness to give the earth enough strength to fight the virus and the accompanying emotions of anxiety and worry.

There were the most obvious activists in the medical field who put their lives at risk to serve those who were infected. Although this was expected of them in their chosen field of work, the unprecedented circumstances demanded that they overreach their call of duty and go beyond expectation. They were no less spiritual in their actions. The medical community mustered all its compassion and service to respond to the call of duty. The other warriors include policemen and service personnel like drivers, delivery executives, and virus contact-tracing specialists in the government who, through their work, kept moving society towards resolution and healing. These are all spiritual warriors.

There was another set of warriors who emerged during this time who were quick to act in the initial days of the crisis to get food and essentials to migrants, daily wagers, and those who were overnight rendered unemployed. Not all of these spiritual warriors were connected to the social service sector. Many of them were working in the corporate or government sectors and felt the strong urge to do their bit and contribute to reduce the pain from the crisis.

Every single person who was responding to the outside world in a positive way became a spiritual warrior. The nature of response matters. From the one who meditated daily to the one who went on the streets distributing food to the jobless and homeless, they were all spiritual warriors.

Spiritual activism converts concern into positive action towards a desired goal.

Social and Spiritual Values

How does a beginner in spirituality know which values are worth fighting for, which ones to keep, and which ones to discard? The generally accepted spiritual values are all human values. They include love, kindness, compassion, peace, non-violence, and so on. But each individual leans towards certain values that she holds in high regard according to her personal understanding of spirituality.

Her path to switching on her inner light could be different from the path used by others. And in alignment with her unique path, she might rate love for animals as a higher spiritual value than, say, peace. She could believe that the way to peace is through equality in love for all beings. Similarly, another seeker could have a spiritual value of nonjudgment and hold this value higher than any other.

Every seeker will eventually find her own set of values to abide by, and from these values, which may or may not intersect with social values, she will build her personal spirituality. The priority of values could also change over time. For example, a seeker may hold the value of respect for elders very high up her list and model her social behaviour to reflect this value. She may take the blessings of elders at social occasions, serve elders, and be there for them. Accordingly, in her activism, she may choose service at old-age homes over every other form of volunteer work.

But with time, her priorities may shift from respect for

elders towards equality. Her life experiences and spiritual journey could make her lean towards equality of all humans irrespective of gender, class, age, and nationality. This mental shift also reflects in her choice of activism. But it is still spiritual activism when the process of achieving the goal takes into account equality in order to reach the ultimate destination.

As a beginner, there is no need to stress too much about listing spiritual values if you are unclear yet. But a good start would be to reflect on the values that you currently hold in high regard and then match your personal spirituality to these values. They will eventually converge through commonalities but the exploration could take you through various routes that shift the priorities of social and spiritual values based on experience. To embrace activism as a form of spirituality, it is essential to be in tune with your personal priority values to do justice to the causes that you choose. If this matching isn't done, there could be internal dissonance leading to disillusionment about the effects of spiritual activism on your emotions as well as on your path.

Spiritual Activism Is Not New

The more fashionable term is spiritual activism. But the concept of giving and charity—of both time and resources—have been around for centuries. The idea now is more organised through professional fundraising and media attention. We know this sector as the social sector, non-profit or not-for-profit work, non-government organisations, charity agencies, etc.

But the spiritual component of this work is extremely individual and is up to the activist to align her spiritual values to the tangible work. Like Jack, the activism can be subdued and powerful, or it could be multi-hued and wide-ranging like Anita's. Either way, the goal is to find ways to take our values and turn them into concrete action for positive results.

Every major world religion has a strong charity component built into the fold. It could be in the form of donations or through service for specific causes.

A beginner spiritual-activist has a choice to associate with a charity through the religious group that she belongs to. This has certain advantages, mainly that a system would already be in place to which the volunteer does the job like a cog in the wheel. For a beginner, this is the most ideal start to the world of activism as she has under control time, a specific job description, and a specific goal.

When I started teaching children from lower-income groups, I started my work through a well-known spiritual organisation. All I had to do was sign up to be a teacher, choose the day of the week I would like to volunteer, and land up at that time. The work was fulfilling and opened my mind to various ideas and thoughts shared by the students as well.

A few years later, a non-profit agency asked me to teach English to slum children near my house. I enjoyed this experience, too, immensely. It was completely different from my experience teaching at the spiritual organisation. Here, on some days there would be many children, and on some others, there would be no children at all. On one occasion, the area coordinator for the agency took me on a walk in the slums where I saw some of the children run away and hide when they spotted the coordinator. She told me that the kids avoided going to school and had to be coaxed into attending class. Their parents, too, weren't invested in the children's education.

The work at the slums demanded a different set of skills that were broader than just teaching a class of students. It required convincing the parents and kids to attend school, and when in class, the students had to be engaged enough to want to return the next day. I did this work for several years, and it was only possible to continue in these volatile circumstances because the work was testing my values of equality and persistence.

I believe that equality can come through education that brings opportunity. And to achieve anything difficult, we must persist through the challenges to emerge successful. These two values, aligned with my personal spirituality, gave me the confidence that I needed to carry on working.

Any activism is for the long haul. In most cases when activists give up, it is usually because their personal philosophy doesn't align with the values that their choice of cause represents. Beginners would do well to ensure this matching right at the beginning.

Also, technology may give us great avenues to explore and choose activism opportunities. But some of the best lessons in giving come from the holy texts and old-school philosophies. It would be wise to lean on ancient wisdom whenever in doubt.

The Spiritual Activism Burnout Trap

Although the aim of volunteer work and giving is to puncture the ego, it can also have the reverse effect. Upon seeing the positive effects that your work has on people's lives, it can make you feel fulfilled at first and, with time, it could also lead to excessive pride and, eventually, a pumped-up ego.

In giving compassion and love to others, the givers

sometimes lose track of the reason they are there. The volunteers also begin to feel that they are responsible for making someone happy and bringing positive lasting change to another's life. This can lead to arrogance and the sense that they are superior to all those who do not do any volunteer work. These tendencies can be brought in check early in the process.

A good way to keep track of this tendency is to regularly check in with oneself while honestly answering the question: How does the volunteer work make me feel? If one notices traces of pride and self-importance, it becomes necessary to remind oneself that this work has, perhaps, become self-serving and is not as selfless as it ought to be. The focus has to be brought back to the cause away from the giver. When the seeker relates non-attachment to the outcome, she is able to control the growing ego as a result of the work.

The other tenet that spiritual activists would be wise to follow is commitment to the process. Any volunteer work is a long-term commitment to the cause. It is not just about one project or one win. It is about being present for the longest and hardest battles in whatever way one can manage. For this to happen, it is essential that the values of the cause align with your personal spiritual values. Only then does the commitment become possible to sustain.

A lot of spiritual learning takes place in the volunteering process. The first valuable lesson is the practice of being non-attached to the outcome of the work while also being emotionally invested in the process. The emotions will play a role in the work, but when it comes to the end result, we are to detach. This is great practice for any aspect of life and work. Karma yoga teaches this attached detachment in which practitioners do every type of work, from cleaning toilets to preparing the company budget with equanimity of emotions. And once the job is done, the seeker detaches from the result so that any outcome, whether praise or criticism, is taken with stoic equanimity of emotions.

The second valuable lesson that spiritual activism teaches is balance. In the various aspects of one's life, including career, family, friends, hobbies, health, and personal spirituality, one can get carried away in volunteer work and use it as an escape from the other aspects of life which may not be going great. Activism is considered 'good' work, therefore, justified as noble in the eyes of society. Activism can become a burden when overdone. When torn between unrealistic commitment and the joy of giving, it can seem justified to continue to do a lot.

It is easy to overcommit time and resources and make volunteering a primary priority. This excessive tilt towards activism at the expense of all other aspects of one's personal life is problematic because, often, the seeker uses time to solve other's problems and not invest adequately in oneself. This is a type of avoidance and running away.

The only way to manage this is to allot time for activism work, and if possible, include it in the time allotted to spiritual work. Adhering to a timetable ensures balance to some extent beyond which the seeker needs to rein in the overenthusiasm.

Signs That You Need to Slow Down on Spiritual Activism

The joy derived from spiritual activism has the power to cloud one's thinking and create imbalance in thought and action. Here are some ways to spot the signs that one needs to re-evaluate the activism work:

1. **Not getting enough rest:** If all your free time is spent on running from pillar to post trying to get things done for an activism project, or if it is draining you out physically and emotionally, it is time for a rethink. When you are not healthy and strong, you will not be in a position to give your best. Take the time to rest and recuperate before you join the group again. Meanwhile, the cause will be taken up by other torchbearers. You should feel comfortable passing the baton when you recognise that it is time for you to rest.
2. **Not having fun:** This is an important criterion, one that is overlooked often because activism carries the aura of seriousness and of bringing joy to sad stories. While this could be true with some causes, it is also important that the activists infuse positive energy and joy to the process of turning around the outcome to a positive one. If you are not having fun as a volunteer, you cannot expect to pass on the cheerful vibe to the cause. If you don't feel motivated to continue with the cause, then check in with your values to see if they still align.
3. **Not agreeing with the path**: You may be enthusiastic about the cause but may not agree with the method chosen to get the desired results. This is another spirituality lesson in which you have the opportunity to practise detachment while doing the assigned work. At the same time, if you feel strongly that the method is unethical or plain wrong, then you should step back and review the nature of work before recommitting to the project. If the method is in direct contrast to your spiritual values, then step

back and continue your commitment to the cause through another project.

4. **Not agreeing with the values**: If your spiritual values clash with the values of the project that you have picked up, then it is best to review your decision. Sometimes, there is joy in the activism even if the values don't match. This is true for short-term projects that don't demand huge investment of time or commitment. But to make a long-term commitment to a project, it is important that the values match.
5. **Not agreeing with the peers**: Activism gets a boost when it is a social engagement that is undertaken with many like-minded activists. The process of learning is enhanced and the activity becomes more enjoyable when one is accompanied by activists who infuse positive energy and strength to the cause, too. Volunteering is often a chosen activity that involves heavy energy exchange. When done alongside peers who believe in the cause as deeply, and have matching values, the two-way benefit is multiplied.
6. **Too attached to people**: It is natural to get emotionally attached to the beneficiaries of the voluntary work. Over time, an emotional connection forms, especially when the foundation of the activism is built on the theme of improving lives. The emotional attachment to people itself is not the problem but the passion for the result of the activism that could make you overreach in the project. Here, this passion is justified as it is for a good cause. But passion is often a short-lived burst of intense energy that is difficult to sustain over a long period of time.

7. **Posturing a moral high ground**: Some of the best human values come together in spiritual activism. You get to offer a leg up to those in need, and in doing so earn a boost of personal spiritual wellness. While this exercise is meant to temper the ego, it could do the opposite by pumping up the ego where you start to feel that you tread a moral high ground compared to others around you, owing to the noble deeds and the visible positive change that you are responsible for facilitating.

Spiritual activism has many life lessons to share. Like Anita, it can be pursued on the go with nothing else but a desire to do something good for others. Anita even detaches from the outcome of all the help that she offers. Or, like Jack, every beginner can carefully choose a cause that is in alignment with her spiritual values and make a long-term commitment to feed that cause with positivity.

Like growing a tree, spiritual activism demands patience, regular care, and watering to watch the seed crack open the soil and grow tall into a living thing. At the end, you may not be the one sitting under its shade or enjoying its fruits. This knowledge should be enough to remove emotional attachment from the project to simply care for the plant with the idea of doing good for the distant future, one in which you may or may not be present.

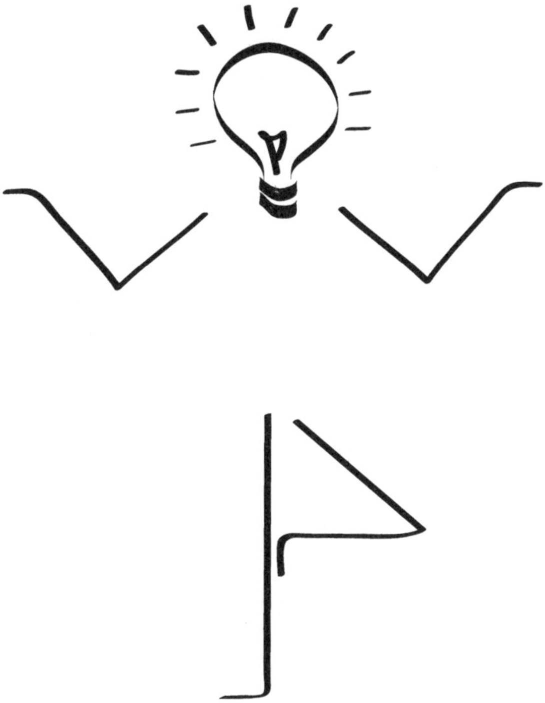

15

The Isolation Myth

'If you are lonely when you're alone, you are in bad company.'

—Jean-Paul Sartre

During my stay at the Sivananda Yoga Vedanta Meenakshi Ashram in Madurai, I met Raj who taught us the Bhagavad Gita. Every other afternoon we would meet to recite verses from the Gita and reflect on its meaning and application to daily life. What struck me as most interesting, a learning that has stayed with me to date, is the attitude of Raj, our teacher.

At around 60 years, Raj looked much fitter and younger. He would join us during our break sessions to crack jokes and talk about everything under the sun. There was no invisible line of difference between Raj and the students as there was with many other teachers, especially the monks.

Raj was a family man and spoke openly about his life at home. He narrated an incident when once his daughter was adamant that she wanted to eat meat. Some of the students listening to this incident were shocked and asked Raj that being a pious man how could he allow meat-eating in his house. Unfazed by the question, Raj answered: 'My daughter wants to eat meat. It is her choice. Why should I have a problem with that? I even chopped some vegetables for her to add to the dish.'

When students would ask questions in class, Raj always answered patiently and with a lightness that expressed his general attitude that one is to smile through life. When we were under stress of the coursework and the difficult daily routine, he would laugh and ask us to not take life so seriously. During the study hour in the evenings, teachers would take turns to monitor students and be available to answer questions. Raj always asked us to be relaxed and allow the information to flow rather than force anything.

When at the ashram, Raj was completely immersed in a yogic lifestyle. When he was back home, he became a family man while still allotting some time for his personal spiritual practice. He contributed time to both aspects of his life, thus, deriving joy out of both.

What appears to be a perfect balance today took Raj years to design, craft, redesign, and practise. Life has a way of throwing even our best-laid plans awry. But a commitment to a desired lifestyle can be made possible through investment of time, effort and, most importantly, determination. Learning how to balance different parts of life is itself both a calculation and an art form. Raj had mastered this and appeared to be at ease with it.

Another person who manages the spiritual life and a public life well is Dr Kashyap. 82-year-old Dr Rangasami L. Kashyap is an unassuming man. Dressed simply in cotton kurta and trousers, with a shawl draped over his right shoulder, he walks slowly given both his age and calm demeanour. He always wears a gentle smile and nods at anyone with a smile of recognition. This gentleman's modest dress betrays the grandeur of his achievements.

Dr Kashyap, a recipient of Padma Shri in 2021 for his contribution to literature and education, is one of India's foremost applied mathematicians who taught electrical engineering at Purdue University for many years. In 1965, he partnered with Yu-Chi Ho to develop the Ho-Kashyap rule, an algorithm for computer pattern recognition and machine intelligence. This achievement aside, Kashyap is now founder-director of Sakshi Trust in Bangalore, a premium institute for study of the Vedas.

For 12 years of his life, Kashyap juggled his university professor's job with translating each of the 25,000-plus Vedic verses from Sanskrit into English, a feat that not many can boast of. Today, he is committed to bringing back the Vedas into everyday Indian lives. It is, to use a cliché, a back-to-the-roots intellectual movement that has practical application to everyday spirituality.

The contrast of a hugely successful public life in the field of applied mathematics and the equally successful spiritual life that now involves teaching and spreading knowledge is rather unusual, and not one that many can manage. But Kashyap's is a story that proves: A public life of fame and recognition and the spiritual life can coexist in harmony. It is up to the person who balances the two, giving each the deserved respect and space in their life. Also, these achievements have not taken away from Kashyap's family life and responsibilities. He is married and continues to fulfil his family dharma, duty towards the family unit.

Primary Responsibility

Beginners would often wonder about the contrasting values that pursuing both a family and spiritual life demand. The former is about fulfilling responsibility towards a partner, parents, children, and family members. Family life is about being present and acting according to the convention that has been passed down through the generations as model behaviour for a family person, generally speaking. It is also true that there are many individuals who design their own definition of a family life and live by their own rules, some of which are in sharp contrast to prescribed popular social expectations. Leading a spiritual life is about devoting time and energy to the pursuit of an inner life that is generally understood in many spiritual traditions to be the ultimate goal of our existence here.

Where do our primary responsibilities lie? In most cases, the choice is already made for us by our circumstances and our readiness to follow the conventional family path. With family life being the default setting in most cultures, the individual is married before she has had the opportunity to fully explore any other form of living. It is only after marriage and the initial life experiences of young-adult life that most of us even open our minds to the possibility of giving space to spirituality.

This is not the stage at which to ask the question: Should I give up family life to pursue spirituality? Once entered into the family fold, it is best that the individual should continue along that path and use the lessons within family life to enhance spiritual living. For beginners, especially, any drastic step like moving out of family life to devote full time to spirituality is both unnecessary and also stands against the very spiritual values that one seeks to imbibe.

Switching on the inner light doesn't necessarily require you to completely sacrifice any other part of your life. In fact, engaging with every part of life and living a full, qualitative existence adds value to the process of turning on the inner light. It is only when one feels ready to engage in a deeper way with her inner light and move towards a committed study and healing work that more time is to be dedicated to the spiritual pursuit.

There are cases in which an individual is drawn towards a spiritual life from a young age and already knows that she wants to embrace this lifestyle. In such cases, forcefully entering family life as it is considered 'normal' is also counterproductive because the individual would be struggling to balance the spiritual and material lives with her energy not fully devoted to either.

When it comes to asking, 'Where does my primary responsibility lie? Is it with the family way of life or with spirituality?' the answer depends on where your intuition leans towards. The idea is to not force any one way of living. Even if one way of life has been chosen, it is fine because the other lifestyle can be integrated into the current one giving you the best of both worlds.

Balancing Spirituality and Family Dharma

Balance is the key to managing both family values and spiritual values. The two values are not mutually exclusive. Some values may even overlap. In most cultures of the world, family duty and responsibility are given top priority. Organised religion is often a part of this world. In many religions, rituals are designed around the family unit to empower the importance of family.

Once immersed in family life, you may be keen to explore spirituality. But there could be a lurking fear that your family life could suffer because of this interest. The general assumption is that spirituality takes you into the depths of your own personality, making you want to spend many hours alone and in isolation while reflecting and ruminating. This image is only a myth and not all spiritual journeys look like this. Although there is potential for much inner work and silence for a spiritual seeker, it does not always necessarily result in withdrawing from social life and primary responsibilities. If this is happening, your family life could be feeling restless because the balance between the spiritual and family lives has gone off-kilter. The introduction of spirituality into your family life has to be done gradually in phases so as not to shock your own inner world and to not shake up your immediate environment.

Withdrawal from family life and the need to go deeper into spirituality happens at the advanced stages of inner work when the seeker feels the need to work with some of the issues that crop up as a result of introspection. Even in such cases, the spiritual work need not upend family life and bring it in the cross hairs of the seeker's spiritual path. It is often a choice made by the seeker and a consciousness to retain the balance between the two parts of her life. In order to maintain the balance, it is essential to understand that the two are not separate. One is part of the other and can be integrated beautifully, in a manner that Raj managed to balance it.

Selling the Idea to the Entire Family

Often, seekers make a social family outing from spiritual events. Once having tasted the benefits of walking the spiritual path, a seeker may feel obliged to introduce her family to the path, sometimes even forcing them to follow the practice. While the intention of sharing the benefits may be noble, the choice of walking a spiritual path or not is every individual's to make, at whatever age or level of maturity.

Many beginners feel that getting the entire family involved in a spiritual organisation, going to satsang together, volunteering together, and sharing a spiritual path will make it less arduous and even justify the balance of spiritual and family dharma. But this rarely works as desired because every person's path is unique and the way in which she navigates to her inner light is also different. A family member may simply not be ready for spiritual work. Or she may not find your recommended spiritual organisation a good fit for her personal spiritual goals.

By taking along the entire family to a satsang, a seeker could take comfort in the fact that there are many people from her family doing similar things but at the individual spirit level; each one is at different points along their own path. Involving the family becomes a social affair and rarely any more than that.

Is Isolation to Be Expected?

Sharing spiritual experiences with family works in the same way that it does when sharing in a social group. It brings the joy of exchange and self-expression but the experiences and path are individual and must be respected as such.

In balancing the spiritual and family life, many seekers—and more often their family members—fear isolation of the seeker. This comes from a rather traditional idea that isolation is bad and that being social is a sign of happiness. This idea cannot be further from the truth.

Much of a beginner-seeker's spiritual work is about learning how to sit still and go inward in search of the inner light. In the process, the seeker is learning about herself and building a relationship with the Self. In many cultures, the practice of sitting still is done in groups as a social activity, often guided by religion.

In general, many have a discomfort or an underdeveloped personal relationship with the Self; hence, they fear it or don't understand its need. There is fear of isolation because our cultures have traditionally not encouraged self-inquiry outside of socially approved templates. Spirituality breaks this mould through its primary tool—meditation. While meditation is increasingly gaining acceptance the world over, close-knit family traditions still fear that a spiritual seeker could stray too far from the family fold while working through advanced spiritual practices.

This is not the case with most beginner-seekers who are learning how to sit comfortably with themselves to build a personal relationship. Extended periods of being in isolation is not a part of the beginner's process unless one chooses to go away to an ashram for a few weeks or months. Reflection and rumination could be some of the side effects of the inner work that require isolation, but it need not be for long stretches of time if the balance is well maintained.

Signs That the Spiritual/Family Life Balance Is off-Kilter

These are the signs to tell if overenthusiasm in pursuing spiritual goals is tilting the balance in the Wheel of Life:

1. **The first sign of the family-spiritual life balance gone awry is that your family members complain about your absence.** If the spiritual work is coming in the way of an important family tradition, like Sunday brunch, that you have had for years, your sudden absence will make things difficult for your family to understand. The only way out is to find

a different time for the meditation work, or to move the family time to later in the day or another day. But try not to cancel the family outing as it is equally important to keep such family traditions. Also, protect your family time and responsibilities—whether it is attending your children's school events or simply keeping up the tradition of game nights. If a family member complains about your absence, it needs to be addressed through investigation about how genuine the complaint is and followed up with action by making adequate amends.

2. **Your family complains of your changed temperament.** This is another sign that there is something amiss. In the course of your meditation or your spiritual inquiry, you could be dealing with difficult emotions or reflecting on life in several ways than before. When doing deep inner work, it is essential to maintain strict boundaries between the inner introspection and the social and familial worlds. When one spills over to the other, especially the intensely powerful emotions within you that need healing, it becomes difficult to manage either. There are ways to mentally and emotionally separate the spiritual work and leave it behind while taking along only the joy, peace, and calm into the family life. The first way is to keep a separate physical space for the work. When you enter the meditation zone, it is your place of calm. When you exit that place, you put a symbolic lock on the issues triggered there while entering the family space again. This is a good energetic hygiene practice to include right from the beginning of your spiritual work. Your revelations

and insights from your meditations are yours alone and shouldn't ideally spill to the other areas of your life.

3. **You feel more withdrawn and prefer to spend more time alone.** Sometimes, the spiritual work may seem heavy, and you would like more time to dissipate the intense energy. It is ideal to ask for a timeout and be by yourself to sort out the triggered emotions. On the other hand, the meditation may be infusing you with positive energy, making you want to spend more and more time in meditation. This is a fair need and must be assessed based on the time already available to you. Ask if your need for more time for spiritual work will impact your family and social life. Not answering this question honestly can lead to the balance of your life going off-kilter in the long run. Be careful about increasing the time spent on spiritual work in incremental raises only, and observe the impact it has on the other areas of your life.
4. **You signed up for a meditation course but don't want to attend.** In enthusiasm, when a friend spoke of the benefits of walking a spiritual path, you signed up for a beginners' meditation course but now feel that you are not ready or that this path is not for you. Simple. Sign out and don't think twice. With any spiritual work, the interest cannot be forced. A lack of interest is often a sign that you are not ready to walk down this path. And there is nothing wrong in it. When you are ready, the path will appear before you. So, it is best to not force anything and allow everything to flow easily in its own time and pace.

If a friend or family member forces you to join a course, you will need to explain to them that you are not ready. They may question your friendship but it doesn't matter. Spirituality cannot be forced.

5. **The other extreme is that you joined a beginners' course and experienced such a life-changing transformation that you are now obsessed with making rapid progress on the spiritual path.** This could happen if a spiritual organisation that you are part of entices you with newer goals and more work with the promise of more benefits. You could feel ready mentally and emotionally, too. But as a thumb rule, it is best to space out all spiritual learning to give yourself enough time to absorb it. The learning and the inner work are not just touching the left brain but are also deeply impacting the right brain, the creative and emotional mind. We may not realise it on the outside but spiritual work has powerful impact on all parts of our consciousness. Pace the learning and go slower than you are ready to learn.

Not Choosing a Family-Centric Lifestyle

While having a family-first lifestyle is a default in a majority of cases, there are many among us who choose to not enter the conventional family set-up and, instead, make their own rules for living. Choosing a non-family-centric life does not naturally make spirituality central to such an individual. Even in such cases, leading a spiritual life is a choice that the individual makes. If the individual has made such a choice of a non-conventional lifestyle and then chooses to make spirituality an important part of it, this person will still need to maintain balance between the different aspects of her life.

Take the example of Susan. Susan decided in her early twenties that she would not like to be married or lead a family life in a conventional way. She works for a large corporate employer and has a full life that is sliced between many of her interests. Career is one aspect of Susan's life. For a long time, Susan has been pursuing long-distance motorbike riding. She is part of a women's motorcycle riding group that organises such trips. This allows her to build a sisterhood that fulfils her passion for riding.

Susan enjoys travel and usually combines her work-related travel with personal journeys around the world. Travel is another aspect of her life that fulfils her need for freedom and is a great reminder, too, that she has chosen a life to be free and not particularly tethered anywhere.

Susan has a religion-led spiritual practice that she has designed based on her interests and needs. She attends church regularly and, through church, gets involved in many social charitable activities. This is her spiritual activism led by the church's priorities. The activism is also her personal spirituality, and she doesn't feel the need to do any more personal spiritual work. She feels that there is enough balance among the different interests of her life, and she is able to make time for each of these.

The important thing here is that Susan enjoys her work and life and is not fussed about what needs to be done or what should be done according to the rules. She has designed her life according to her personal values. These values intersect with her spiritual values, and it makes her choices easy to follow.

There are others who choose a spirituality-first lifestyle in a clear move away from the family-centric life. Such seekers in most cases have a broad idea of how they want their spiritual path to unfold. This kind of lifestyle still requires balance and a connection with every part of one's life.

Not only is the switch from the family life to spiritual life a theme but so is its reverse, although not that common. In the 1990s, an ordained monk of a religious order in South India, after decades of being a monk, fell in love with one of his disciples and chose to give up sainthood to marry. Overnight, the followers of that religious sect who fell at this monk's feet to seek his blessings were now standing shoulder to shoulder with him and shaking hands. He embraced the spiritual-to-family life switch as, perhaps, there was a need within his soul to experience that side of life.

Any kind of switching sides comes from being convinced that it is in your best interest. You can, however, soften the blow of a drastic and sudden shift by paying incremental attention in time and resources to the various parts of your life so that you detect the need for a tilt early on and feed that requirement. It requires staying centred and grounded to every need and, then, fulfilling the ones that your heart calls out to.

Ways to Maintain a Balance between Family Dharma and Spiritual Calling

Here are a few ways to practise being at the centre of the Wheel of Life:

1. **Being present in the moment:** Being in the here and now is a lesson that is taught by many spiritual greats as the answer to almost all of life's miseries that crop from the mind. Thinking of the past

brings sorrow and worrying of the future brings anxiety. Only being in the present erases the mind's rapid fluctuations. Be in the meditation fully and thoroughly while in the practice. When at a family dinner, be there fully and thoroughly giving of your mind and body in total attendance. Thinking of all the things that you haven't done for family during meditation time is not serving any purpose. It isn't helping you get more time for family, nor is it optimising your meditation time.

2. **Being comfortable with imperfection:** The game of balance is about doing anything that we do to the best of our ability while leaving the nitpicking to others. Any juggling act requires some level of letting go. A homemaker-cum-career woman may have to sacrifice the shape of her rotis in favour of squeezing in a morning meeting from home. A seeker who is helping his son with a school project may have to spend less time at the garden with the plants. But each one is still present and doing the best they can. And this is all that matters.

3. **Running the marathon:** We indulge in all the important parts of life and work keeping in mind that they are for the long term. They are not short sprints in which we make a dash for the finish line. With life, we don't even know where the finish line is; with spirituality, there probably is no finish line. Treat all work as daily practice for a race somewhere in the vague future. Then make incremental improvements to your life by adding to its quality by shaping and designing tasks to your need. In short, go slow and steady while breathing evenly.

4. **Staying at the centre:** Tilting too much in favour of one part of life at the expense of all others is problematic because it could topple your balance. Find ways to feed every need in different ways. These could be your own unconventional ways or you could choose society-approved conventional ways to enhance the balance of your life. But the balance is important, and it will determine your mental and emotional peace— also physical health, too—in the long term.
5. **Having fun in every part of life:** Fun is underrated in the spiritual process and in the larger move towards achieving better life balance. If you are not enjoying what you do or are unhappy with some part of your life, make a conscious effort to improve it for the better. If a spiritual path is not fun anymore, move to another that seems to align with your interests. It is the same with life and work. Fun, laughter, and joy are integral parts of our life and must be given their due. Only then will life seem worth living.

Conclusion

When I reflect on what my personal spirituality has looked like in the past decades, there is not one single enduring image that comes to mind. In fact, it is a sea of images that flood my mind's eye in a flash of a few seconds, overlapping and zooming through my attention span.

It includes trekking in the mountains, stretching on the yoga mat, making a clay Ganesha, writing when I was not in the mood, partying hard till the morning, walking out of a relationship, being disciplined about achieving a personal goal, sitting in meditation, feeling disappointed in a friend, and living the beauty of the human touch. Every moment was an opportunity to care less about the things that don't matter and to care more about the things that do matter . . . all with awareness. I did well sometimes and didn't on many occasions.

I read a quote about spirituality that I don't remember verbatim. But let me paraphrase here: Spirituality isn't the image of sitting cross-legged on the floor in a clean room with meditation music on, wearing a serene expression of contentment. It often looks like slipping, skidding, and rolling down the forest hills, getting bumped and thrown along the way to arrive with torn clothes, aching muscles and bruises but with lessons well learned.

My spirituality has been about realising how wrong I was about so many things that I thought I knew. It has been about accepting that I know so little, and then learning to expect even less because life doesn't turn out the way we expect it to. And if it did, what a boring life that would be!

It is the inner light that shows the way to what we know and don't know, mostly about ourselves. This is the real process of discovery, one that's daunting considering how many of us run away from the self, unable to face what we already know. Spirituality is about holding us down to look ourselves in the mirror and accepting the truth.

One often wonders if there is a goal to arrive at in one's spiritual pursuit. Is there a tangible destination, which, when reached, assures us of having arrived correctly where we are supposed to?

The answer is both simple and complex. The simple answer is no, being spiritual is not necessarily about reaching a destination or arriving somewhere. The complex answer is that it is, rather, a way of life that one chooses so that one can live with greater awareness. In that, every tiny milestone of choosing peace over conflict, kindness over meanness, and love over hate is a destination.

By switching on the inner light, a seeker who has chosen to include spirituality in her life will be able to understand the Self better, understand her environment and the world around her while consistently adding to what she knows and how she feels. This understanding will, then, prompt her to move towards greater healing and to make choices with awareness.

Some spiritual paths do dangle goalposts and destinations, some of which are easier to reach than others. The different spiritual pathways interpret the journey and the destination in unique ways. The tantric tradition believes that when we have let go of karmic baggage, the soul becomes light as a feather. We are then ready to merge with the light source, the *Parashakti*. In Hindu traditions, the cycle of karma has no beginning or end. It is an endless cycle where our actions and behaviour determine how we free ourselves from the karmic entanglements. In some other traditions, there is nothing beyond what we experience in this world. Heaven and hell are right here, and we live it all in this one lifetime.

Whatever the belief and however one chooses to approach the spiritual path, the work of switching on the inner light is about achieving balance, which is a deeply individual pursuit. No one else can define it for us, nor can they live it for us. Even if there is no greater goal to achieve by switching on the inner light, it serves the purpose of accepting our life here, thereby improving it.

What, then, determines if we are on the right path and if we are making progress? A teacher once told me that no matter what, we are always on our path. If we are drawn to one type of meditation over another, it is our path. If we are drawn to a cult, it is our path. If we are drawn to explore other groups and techniques, again, it is because we are already on our path. Our only job is to keep moving and to partner with our inner light . . . allowing it to lead us.

The spiritual path rarely ever looks the same for any two people. Not everyone may understand our journey, and it is not for them to understand either. Spirituality is about me understanding my journey and supporting myself along my unique path.

Much of spirituality is celebrated in the intangible. Every seeker's parameters to measure these intangibles would differ. I do this qualitative test by simply asking myself: Do I care more for the things that are important to me? And do I care less about the things that are not important? In other words, this is the process of investing in the people and emotions that make us feel better and letting go of the things that chip away at our peace of mind. Spirituality, in large part, is about making these choices of what's important and what's not. And if we are able to make these choices with kindness, compassion, and grace, it means that we are getting closer to working in partnership with our inner light. And our ability to know if we are doing these things well can be revealed to us when our own inner light is switched on and shines on our life's journey.

As you embark on your personal journey, mentally prepare for a marathon in which you are allowed to rest, take breaks, and deviate to take a more scenic road. But keep moving forward. When you wear the spiritual lens, the world looks more meaningful and more fun, too. Here's wishing that your inner light brightens your whole world, reaching far and wide.

Have a safe and beautiful journey!

AUTHOR'S THANKS

I HAVE IMMENSE GRATITUDE TO THE FOLLOWING people without whom this book would not have seen the light of day.

Prashant Sankaran: My best friend, writing partner, drinking buddy, and collaborator of good and bad, excellent and awful ideas. Thank you for encouraging me to write this book. You teach me every day how to live with compassion and kindness.

Chaitanya Sridhar: One of the first readers of the manuscript, a fellow-seeker par excellence, and a humanist above all else. Your feedback was invaluable in turning around the first draft.

Sonali Pawar: Your deft editing has lent grace and flow to the words. You are a writer's dream come true.

Ashok Chopra: Thank you for seeing the light in this book and allowing it to reach the readers.

Vinay Kamat: An editor and friend that I respect and admire; your feedback filled me with confidence and assurance.

Vivek Kaul: Thank you for making room for me to air my crippling self-doubts and then throwing them out the window to let the sunshine in. It is always a pleasure to share writing notes with you.

Sairica Rose: My sister from across the seas. You kick me in the butt and make me see life upside down if that's what is needed. I learn from you every day.

Lisa Leonard: Fellow seeker, empath, and healer; you make me feel understood. Thank you!

Sachin Sharma: A friend without whom this book would not have been possible. You also magically bring the right words of encouragement to prod me on. Thank you!

Deepa Tekur: My sister and partner in crime and spirituality, fellow seeker, gossip buddy, and notes sharer. You make life colourful! Thank you for lending your creative touch to the illustrations at the start of each chapter.

Shirdinath and Vijayalakshmi: My parents who stood witness, in bewilderment and amusement, to all of my life's disappointments and successes. Without you, I am nothing.

Arun Bhat: Thank you for being patient with me as I fussed to get before the camera for the author pic.

All my teachers from around the world on the spiritual and material paths: Everywhere I go, I carry around the flame of curiosity that you lit in me.

All the fellow seekers that I crossed paths with: Many of you have played a starring role in the book's anecdotes. I learned so much from you.

All the guys who brought love and romance into my life: Our stories may be over, but you played an important part in shining my inner light. Thank you!

I am eternally grateful!